THE MIRACLE

BY

JAY NEYENS

The Miracle

by

Jay Neyens

ISBN 13: 9781088044254 – Paperback
ISBN 13: 9781088044315 – eBook

Neither the author nor the publisher assumes any responsibility or liability whatsoever on behalf of the consumer or reader of this material. Any perceived slight of any individual or organization is purely unintentional. The resources in this book are provided for informational purposes only and should not be used to replace the specialized training and professional judgement of a health care of mental health care professional.

Neither the author nor the publisher can be held responsible for the use of the information provided within this book. Please, always consult a trained professional before making any decision regarding treatment of yourself or others.

TO THE HEROES

No one expects their life to change in an instant and to be put into the hands of some of the most amazing and compassionate people ever.

They call them the helpers, but when you experience their care, you will call them heroes.

These are people that can't turn away, don't run in other direction and make sure they do the best they can to care for their fellow humans.

I was touched by some amazing people, and I hope that somehow karma will enrich their lives like they did mine.

I need to again give special thanks to Hannah, my physical therapist. You played such an important role in my journey and still play an amazing part in my recovery. Thanks, my friend.

THE MIRACLE

My name is Jay Neyens.

I am originally from a small town in the Midwest called Dubuque, Iowa. Sorry, I laughed a little when I wrote that. Seems so long ago. It was the kind of place where your parents instilled great values and work ethic, and the people are so friendly and helpful, it was a great place to be born and raised.

I was a singer at a very early age and played in local bands, I knew that this would be my path in life. I would need to be creative to survive and prosper in my life. I moved to Los Angeles, California with some friends when I was 18. I knew I would have to make the hard choice in my life: to sacrifice being with my family in a small town or move to a large city where I knew there was a real opportunity for me to make a difference in the music and entertainment business. As I was quick to learn, a lot of this business is being in the right place at the right time and having the wherewithal to take advantage of the opportunity.

And a little luck never hurt.

But it seemed I had some of those things going for me after I graduated from The Vocal Institute, a musicians institute in Los Angeles. I got an award for outstanding vocalist of the year, not because I was a great singer, but I was a great student. I put in 100 percent, and this was before the internet and shows like American Idol. This was during the time you had to really work at your craft and play as much as you could. The Sunset Strip was my office for many years, and I was lucky to play with some amazing musicians and make some great music.

During my journey, I was lucky enough to meet a guy who would change my life. He and his family were very successful in the special effects business in Hollywood. They were nice enough to take me under their wing and teach me the business. They did wind, rain, and fire explosion for the film and TV industry. We worked on some of the biggest films, TV shows and music videos. We worked with everyone from Snoop Dog to Michael Jackson. Some days I couldn't believe where I was and what I was doing. It was amazing. For a young kid from Iowa, I was living my best life.

After years of the high stress and fast pace of the entertainment business, my family – twins Zack and Josh, and their mother, Mariam - decided to move. We wanted a new state that would be a little less stress, a little less traffic. So, we landed in Arizona. It was great. Mariam stayed in the music business as a music promoter and I took a year off to recover from getting hurt on the last movie I worked on, *Blade*, where I broke my knee.

Fast forward 20 years. I am divorced amazing twin boys who are the youngest twin inventors in the USA, a title they've had since they were six years old. Now they are 19 and I am 56. I help run their business and do artwork and still sing. I am super busy with lots going on in my life. I am best friends with the boy's mother and, as you can see, I have been so lucky in my life. I've had some amazing experiences and just when you think it can't get any better…

…it doesn't.

CHAPTER ONE: THE EVENT

Seemed like a typical summer morning, that Sunday, August 15th. I was getting ready to go Door Dash to make some extra cash while my paintings dried, like I typically did every Sunday morning. And yes, anyone who suffers a traumatic event will normally remember the time and date that it happened. I guess it's part of the scar you have.

I liked to get started early in the morning, that way, my run is done by early afternoon. Normally on Sundays, I would head to my boy's house after making my run to hang out with them and have a good Sunday with the family. If I can, I always like to work around my neighborhood and around the boy's house. That way, I'm there for them if they need anything, or after work, it's easy for me to get to them. I live and work in the Arrowhead suburb of Glendale, Arizona. It's a nice area to work and a great area to live, and this was a busy morning. Once I was finished with my runs, I wanted to grab breakfast and head over to the boy's house. My twin boys just turned 19 years old, and they live with their mom, Mariam.

In August in Phoenix, it's usually hot. After grabbing my breakfast, I rolled up my windows and headed to the boy's house through a neighborhood near them. I was going through a green light on Deer Valley Rd. off 59th Ave. It was 10:30 on that Sunday morning when I was T-boned at that intersection by drunk driver. He went through the red light at a high rate of speed, hit me and then bounced off two other cars before it was over.

Luckily, I don't remember very much from the accident. I don't remember getting hit at all. I just remember choking on my teeth as they were cutting me out of my car. The noise was so loud. They managed to cut me out of my car, put me on a backboard, and I heard someone say, "Grab his ID. He will be DOA."

I remember trying to think what that means again, *DOA?* then I passed out. I did wake up again for a brief moment in the emergency room. I heard someone say, "He woke up, but he's nonresponsive," and I remember thinking, *No, I'm here. Save me, please, save me*. I also remember thinking, *Oh my god, I am in the hospital. Why I am here? What is happening?* Then I passed out again and I would not have a conscious moment for the next month. My body started the fight of its life.

Meanwhile, the police were in desperate search for my next of kin. They came to my house and my two dogs were barking at the door. They went to the front office and asked management if they had any info on me for my next of kin. After finding the address for my ex-wife and kids, they ran to break the news of my accident.

ꕥ

Mental note: always make sure everyone knows who your emergency contact person is and always have that information written down where someone can find it.

ꕥ

There was precious time lost trying to find out who I was and who I matter too. So, imagine you open the door and it's the police. They are there to explain your loved one was in a bad car accident, and you need to rush to the hospital. This was the worst day ever for my family.

My family rushed to the emergency room to be with me and try to get a grasp on what had just happened to me. Because I'm divorced, my sons were placed as power of attorney so that they could start to make all financial and medical decisions on my behalf.

When I was 19 years old, my dad died of cancer and my boys knew that. Now, here they are, 19 years old, and their dad's about to die. If they weren't grown up before, they were about to be.

ᘓᘕ

Unfortunately, I would be unable to comfort them as I spent the next three weeks in the ICU in a coma, paralyzed from the neck down, oh yeah, with pneumonia on a ventilator. But it was my family that had it the hardest. Let's face it, no one wants to have to put their kids in a position to make life saving decisions for their parent, but here we were. The boys were currently working the night shift at the local Krispie Kreme donut shop, so they would sleep all day and work all night. My son Zack would ask the doctors and surgeons to call him by 9:00 o'clock in the morning so that he could go to bed and get sleep for the day.

After I was in recovery, it was hard to hear him tell me that he was afraid he would make the wrong decisions, of what surgeries to do and what actions to take to help me survive. He told me he would always just say to them, "I guess you've been doing this a long time. I trust your advice on what's best for my dad." That part made me laugh, but deep down I felt very guilty for putting him in that position. I also remember how proud I was at that moment when he told me that.

I also felt so bad for his twin brother, Josh, who once he saw me in the emergency room, was unable to come back and see me in that condition. He supported his brother and mom, helped take care of the dogs and helped our family deal with this tragedy in his own way. Imagine you're 19 years old and the doctor hands you a box of all of your dads' stuff, the clothes he was wearing and all of his belongings. No wonder he couldn't come back to see me. I feel so bad he had to go through that experience.

My injuries were very extensive. In order to live, I had to undergo five major surgeries. Just some of those injuries included a brain injury, a broken neck, broken collarbone, many broken ribs, broken hips and brain injuries. Also, tons of internal injuries took out my spleen, cut part of my liver, bruised heart, bruised lungs, collapsed arteries and many, many other injuries. The doctors had to rebuild my stomach twice. All of these surgeries were done within the first three weeks I was in the ICU.

It was around the third week one of the doctors called Zack and said, “Right now, your dad only has a little movement in his feet, but nothing in his arms or upper body. But I think I can do a surgery that might help take the pressure off his spinal cord.” Of course, Zack couldn't wait to sign me up and I'm glad he did.

Remember, there are always two realities going on in my world during this process: what my family is going through, and what I am going through. I have not yet been introduced to my new reality because I have been out this whole time.

Keep in mind when you are in a traumatic car accident, especially for the type of injuries that I had, you are on a lot of heavy medications, pain killers and other drugs with a room full of machines that are basically keeping you alive. I found that during that first six weeks, I had a lot of illusions, mistrust, and sporadic behavior as I became aware of what happened to me.

However, what happened next had me rethinking religion, miracles, faith and life itself. Whether this was a dream, an illusion or near-death experience, I'm not sure, but for me it seemed real.

You be the judge; here's how it went down. I believe this experience happened during my next surgery, but I am not certain. It seemed like I was in my hospital room

I felt someone sit down on the end of my bed. I lifted my head to see who it was and there was my mom on the bed. Now, keep in mind, my mom had passed away four years earlier. When I was a kid, she used to call me Charlie, I think, after my uncle Chuck.

She said, “Hello Charlie.” She looked like she was 45 years old. She was beautiful with dark hair. She looks so happy. She said, “I think it's time to come home, Charlie.”

I looked at her and said, “I can't mom. I have the boys and they need me.”

She said, “I know honey, but your vessel is so broken.”

When she said that, I remember in my dream or experience, I looked down my arms and the hair was standing up on them. t freaked me out a little because I thought, *Why did she call it a vessel? It's my body*. In that moment, I thought, *Wow, what if this is real and I'm really about to die?*

Then she said, “You have so many injuries. It will take so long to recover, and I know you don't like that.”

I said, “I can't, mom. I have to stay with my boys.”

She said, “Okay, but next time you won't get the choice.” She said, “I will try to leave you with a gift.”

I remember thinking, *Okay, what?* and as soon as I finished that thought in my head, I saw her start to disappear back into the other gray shadow sort of light. Later in the book, I will explain other illusions, dreams or experiences I had and why this one seemed so different.

ଷ୍ଠ

The next day, they started to bring me out the coma. They had to do this throughout the three-week period. I would go in and out of a coma according to how my body was able to take the pain. My family said during this time I was never awake, yet I would make the sign of the cross over and over, and if they asked me a question or talk to me, I would just make the sign of the cross. I was brought up Catholic and went to church until my brother Doug could drive. Then we just said we were going and went to the donut shop.

But my son Zack was like, "Mom? What is dad doing with his hands?"

She said, "It must be from his Catholic up bringing when he was a kid."

Finally, after three weeks, the worst of it was over. Thank God they didn't pull the plug. Listen folks, always have a plan and make sure you have your final wishes down in writing so that your loved ones will always know what to do in this type of situation. This was a valuable lesson. Every person is offered a life but there's no guarantee when the expiration date of that life comes due. Make sure you make the decision of what will happen so that your family it's not left trying to figure it out.

Okay, so there it is. Much to everyone's surprise, I lived. It was time to wake me up as much as they could so that we could determine the final damage and try to prepare me for recovery rehabilitation and move me to a new hospital to start that process.

CHAPTER TWO

As I begin to recover, there are two components that I need to factor in at this point: how my mind and my body will now begin to recover differently. How well those two components recover are based on how bad my injuries were and how determined I am to get better.

At this point I'm still in the emergency room in a North Phoenix hospital after being put back together by some of the best surgeons in the city. They're about to move me to a new location. Mentally, I still have no idea what happened to me, and even though people are talking to me and explaining I've been in a car accident, it does not register, and I just want to go home. I really only remember them moving me to a new location via transportation in an ambulance. They came to get me, and the guys were very nice and explained to me I was heading to another hospital in South Phoenix where I could begin to recover.

I could not speak. I just made noises and used my hands to communicate. I remember falling asleep a lot as we traveled down what seemed like endless hallways. I specifically remember them wheeling me out into a parking lot and how hot it was at night. I was so cold for so long and now here I was finally warm. I remember one of the nurses saying, "I bet this feels good, huh?" I remember nodding my head and as she grabbed my hand to say goodbye, she said, "You're gonna be just fine. I know it."

They loaded me into the ambulance, and I was off to my next adventure, not realizing this would be the hardest year of my life. Keep in mind at this point I'm still on heavy medications and had many tubes coming out of my body and many machines keeping me alive.

ଷଓ

Once I arrived at my new location I was brought to the Level 1 trauma unit at a very large hospital. I was checked in and assigned to my room. Remember rooms are expensive so you always get a roommate. I have to say I don't really remember too much of my first week there. I was on heavy painkillers and was now feeling the pain of my many injuries. I know that I had a lot of family and friends around but still cannot recall any of that interaction. I just knew I kept wanting to go home. I could also tell there was some type of very regimented schedule going on around me with many nurses and doctors coming to see me, and I started to be aware of daytime and nighttime and I specifically remember always hating the nighttime.

I am still on a feeding tube with many other tubes and machines hooked up to me. I can barely move parts of my body, but I can feel the severe injuries. Nights were the worst because that's when everything hurt the most. You're always feel uncomfortable. Keep in mind, I have a broken neck with a neck brace, many broken ribs, a broken collarbone, a broken hip…there was no shortage of pain. Every night I had to sleep on my back and could not move.

☙❧

At night, all you could hear were people screaming in pain, screaming for help. "Get me out of here. Let me go home, I need a nurse, please help me."

I was one of them. I have been taken me off the ventilator, but I still had a trach in my throat. I couldn't scream as loud as those other people, but I was screaming. They were slowly taking me off the heavy painkiller medications and what a ride that was. I had many hallucinations and remembered some of the craziest things about that moment in time. It was like watching a movie.

Like when my sons would come to visit. I thought they worked for the hospital. I remember thinking I was sitting on a couch with two people I didn't like and when the boys would come in the room, they were in lab tech coats. and I would say. "Hey guys, what's up?"

They would say, "Nothing. Just working on some new medicine so that we can get you out of here."

And I would always say, "Hey, get me off this couch," and they would say, "Maybe later dad." I remember how much that pissed me off. LOL.

When you are living hour to hour, you have no concept of reality. Somehow, I knew I was getting better. I must admit it seemed like this moment in time lasted forever it seemed so long.

After the second week in my new location, I realized this was a very large hospital and one that trained people to in this field of work. First, let me say I have high admiration for everyone in the medical field. I would find the next couple of weeks very challenging when it came to being a pincushion for new recruits. This is where I realized that the people that enter this profession have a career and are some of the most caring, giving, and understanding individuals that God created. And then there are some people that just needed a job and ended up taking care of me, which soon led to some very tough life lessons for me.

During the day, I was starting to have moments of very good clarity and understanding, and that's when my ex-wife, Mariam, who, by the way, turned out to be my biggest hero of all, told me the news. She explained to me that I had been in a severe car accident. She said I was hit by a drunk driver in the neighborhood by her house, that the gentleman went through a red light, and T-boned me. She didn't go into full detail but explained that I was hurt very bad. I remember the first thing I said was, "Are you sure it was not my fault? There was nothing I did that caused this accident?"

She replied, “No. You didn't even see it coming.

For some reason, I remember feeling a huge relief. I knew that all of this must be costing a ton of money and I just wanted to make sure that I was not responsible for this. And I remember thinking the irony of a guy who never drank alcohol almost getting killed by a drunk driver.

She continued to say, “All you need to worry about is getting better. I'll take care of everything else.”

It's weird, but I never trusted someone so much in my life as I did at that moment. I knew that I was hurt bad and that I would have to trust that her and the boys would get me back home.

I tried to get used to my new daily routine: people changing, bandages, checking my IVs and machines, cleaning my wounds, and getting my medications. But I also started to notice something else. It was the smell of food. Every day they would deliver food and drinks to my roommate. The smell was amazing, and I started to realize it had been weeks since I had a drink of water or anything to eat. I asked my nurse, "Can I have something to eat?" and she said, "You've been eating all day. You have a feeding tube so you're not ready yet for solid food."

This was a huge disappointment and reality check for me. I was injured so bad I could not even eat real food. This would be the first of many reality checks that would lead me to where I am today.

Never take for granted what you have and what you were able to do because tomorrow, all those things could be gone.

As a couple days went by, I was starting to get a better grasp on daytime and nighttime. I realized I saw a lot of my doctors during the day. They were all very happy to see me and very excited to see that I had lived. They all called me "The Miracle." They said they could not believe that once

I woke up how quickly I was healing. I would always smile and give them a thumbs up.

Still, I could not speak. I could only wave my hands, move my eyes and try to get people to understand what I wanted. This was also the first time I remembered my best friend George coming to visit me even though he had been there many times through the whole thing. He gave me a white board to write on to make it easier for me to communicate. He said he would ask me a question and I would respond with a squiggly line on my whiteboard and just open my eyes real wide like, “You get it, right?” LOL.

Even the boy’s mom couldn’t figure out what I was writing. I used to get so mad when I would scribble and look at her like, “Read it, damn it!” LOL.

I was wiped out. They were trying so hard. They were so patient with me and helped me wrap my head around what had happened. My buddy George even brought his guitar to the hospital to play some tunes for me and the other patients, but I don't remember. He tried everything to make me better, but mostly we both laughed. I can't explain the gratitude I have for him and his wife, and other close friends and family that seemed to have wrapped their arms around me so tight at this point in my life. I realize that during recovery, the most important thing you need is support from your friends and family. You need to know you are loved in order to want to live.

Like I said before, there were always two realities going on: mine and my family's. I had a whole life going before this happened, so it was up to my family to try to not only juggle their lives but try to maintain mine as well. This included heading to my house every morning to pick up my dogs, taking them back to their house where they were fed and let out through the day, and then bringing them back to my house every night so they could sleep in their normal environment.

This is an easy favor to do once in a while, but this went on for three months. Recovery takes family. It takes all the strength and dedication wanting you to get better. Not only is everyone living their normal lives, but now they are helping with everything they can plus visiting you and taking care of bills for you…really anything and everything it takes. I have a newfound respect for all my friends and family and appreciate everything they have done to get me to the point I'm at now.

Like I said earlier, this hospital I was in also trains people to be in the medical field. Even though I'm in full support of this, I do realize now how it sometimes it affects patience. I remember one night a young girl coming to my room telling me she had to take blood like they did every couple of nights. I said, "Okay," and she preceded to try at least five times to hit my vein. Finally, I said, "Okay. I'm done. Why don't you send a phlebotomist by in the morning, and she'll get my blood."

She explained it doesn't always work that way, but she would see what she could do. I said, "I appreciate that, but I know for tonight, we're done. Thank you." This was the first time I realized that in order to get better and get out of here, I would have to become my own advocate. I was also starting to speak and think with a clearer head, and I started to realize that my mind was healing faster than my body. I remember laying there in my bed at night listening to all the screams in the hallway. It would scare the hell out of me; it sounded like I was in a psych ward. People yelling for help, some guy yelling that somebody was trying to kill him, and people were after him, and even my roommate screaming in pain. I always remember thinking, *Damn am I going to lose my mind like that*. You are just never sure what's going on.

ஐ

TIP #1: BODY SCANNING

When I was growing up and was a young musician looking for jobs, I took a side gig working for a hypnotist friend from my small town in the Midwest. This guy was amazing at what he did and traveled all over the country doing shows. For a brief moment, I drove him to his different shows, and I would help him set up. During this time, he taught me self-hypnosis and he said, “You can use this tool for almost anything you need in your life.” And over the years, I’ve used that tool many times.

Now I was gonna use it to help heal myself at night when I went to bed. I would lay there and get myself into a very relaxed state. Your body heals when your mind is in the Alpha state. I would count back from 10 with my eyes closed and then I would call up my army. That army was many little steel workmen that, in my mind, I would send to work every night in a different area to heal the many different problems that I had. It was as simple as saying, “Hi guys. My hip has been really hurting lately and tonight, I want everyone to that location to work on the pain, inflammation, and healing in that spot.” I would spend the next couple of minutes imagining them shooting through my veins to that location and explaining the goals I wanted to achieve, healing, less pain, repair bones, no infections.

Then I would fall asleep and let them work. Every day when I woke up, the area I sent them to felt a little better. Every night, I would repeat this process to the many different locations that needed help. The more I did this, the more it would help. The mind is a very powerful and unique piece of machinery. It can be used to heal you at much faster rate.

Even though I was still only a couple weeks into my new location, I was starting to feel a little better. And I was learning that I still must fend for myself. I was trying to understand the system and, of course, push the limits so I could get what I needed to get out of there.

But, as I found one night, it did not work out for me. I was in a lot of pain and every night when I went to sleep, my neck would start to kill me. So, like every other night, I would have to push the button. No one would show up. I'd scream and yell for help and no one would show up. I get that there were a lot of patients to take care of and I'm sure the time that went by was not as long as I thought it was, but this particular night, I couldn't take it anymore.

My room was next to the break room. I could hear the nurses talking during their lunch break around 1:00 in the morning. After many calls for help, I saw a small bottle on my table. I thought if I threw that bottle against the wall surely they would hear me and come help. LOL. I have to say I never anticipated what was about to happen. I threw the bottle against the wall, and it made a loud bang. Three people came running in my room.

They said, "What happened?"

I said, "I've been yelling for help for an hour now and no one has come to help me, so I threw that bottle against the wall to get your attention."

From there a young female nurse said, "Well you can't do that and now you're gonna be sorry." They proceeded to put these very small, tight gloves – mittens really – on my hands. Then they tied me down to my bed. They tied my legs down as well. I was so confused. I couldn't believe what was happening.

I said, "What are you doing? I'm just asking for help." No one said a word. They just continued to tie me down and then left.

I realized after about four hours being in that situation that no one was coming back to save me. By this time, I had peed myself at least twice and was exhausted from no sleep. When the day nurse walked in, she said, "Oh no. What happened?"

I said, "I think I had a bad night.

She said, "It looks like it," then proceeded to untie me, clean me up, and explain how important it was I don't throw things. All I could do was laugh. I thought, *Where the hell am I? In prison or in a hospital?* It was hard for me to wrap my head around what had happened the night before. But I was so happy to wake up each day, I just moved on to the next challenge.

By now, instead of living by the hour, I'm feeling a little better and starting to live by the day. Each morning they would tell me what procedures I would have that day or what doctors were coming to see me or what scans or x-rays I needed to do. I was communicating better but starting to realize that I can't take care of myself at all. Nurses have been combing my hair, brushing my teeth, doing all kinds of things to me I didn't think I would let nurses do. This was tough for me. I have always been an independent, able person. Now there was so many things I couldn't do. This would have to be a new beginning. I was committed. The better I felt, the faster I wanted to heal. I could feel it each day, my brain reconnecting my body and coming back to life.

They say, "No pain, no gain." They weren't kidding. With every doctor visit, it seemed like I was heading in the right direction. I kept thinking about something every doctor would say to me. They would say, "Man, you are so positive and have such a great sense of humor about what has happened to you."

I would say, "I can't change what happened to me before I woke up. I can only take control of where I'm at now so I can get where I want to be. Quite honestly, I'm just glad to be alive.

CHAPTER THREE

TIP #2: POSITIVE OUTLOOK

I know this one is tough and seems like it has no place in this scenario but being positive will turn out to be the main ingredient in my success as a patient. There are so many hurdles to get over at this point to hit my end goal. If I concentrate on the negative and the pain and the suffering and the "why me," those thoughts will consume my actions and will affect my outcome of being healthy. I can only concentrate on the good things and the positive people that are helping me and loving me and encouraging me to recover. The way I think is the way I feel, so you have to stay positive through your traumatic situation. It's not easy and it is a roller coaster, but you have to always try to keep yourself positive and those around you positive for the best outcome. People want to help those who want to be helped.

ஐ

As I enter, like, week three in the new location, I am more aware. My mind is coming back the quickest and I am starting to realize that every interaction I have with a nurse, or a doctor is a test. Not only are they making sure that my injuries are healing but that my mind is also recovering.

As soon as I got a handle on this, I tried to remember everyone's name who came in my room. Doctors, nurses even my roommate's guest. When I would see them again, I would always call them by name. This not only helped my brain recover but it made them feel like I was mentally sound. Again, I listened to the people screaming in pain and having delusions every night. It scared the hell out of me. Every day, I wanted to seem as mentally stable as possible because I didn't know if they gave those people drugs that made them that way.

By this time, I have a new roommate, a nice guy who had a stroke and heart attack, I think. At night, and all night, he would speak in a weird language he made up. It was a trip. But after a while, I think I started to understand that dude. The nurse would say to him, "Sorry, I don't know what you're saying."

I would yell over, "He wants more water." LOL.

And she would say, "Oh. LOL."

I also remember my first physical therapist asked me what type of music I like. I said rock music.

He said, "Like Bon Jovi?"

I said, "Yeah," and named off like three songs. LOL. When he left, I heard him say to the nurse, "That dude seems pretty sound to me. He named off some songs. Seems like his memory is coming back."

I remember thinking, *Nice work.* LOL

At this point, I am off super heavy meds and down to pain maintenance which means I need to tell them I am in pain to get something to help me. The pain is at its worst during this whole experience. I am in a very uncomfortable bed with a neck brace. Roll over or move and the pain was like an out of body experience.

And I know it's weird, but everyone should feel that because it makes feeling good so much more amazing. I still really don't have a grasp on how badly I was hurt. I just know most of my body hurts. I lay there wondering what could be wrong with me and who the hell has, like, 10 doctors come to see them.

I did have a room with a view. I always kept the window open to let the sunshine on me during the day and always ask everyone if they would take me outside so I could sit in the sun. They always said, "Someday." Even my family. LOL. They explained

I was hooked up to too many machines at the moment. I was always trying to plan my escape, but it never worked, mostly because I couldn't get out of bed to save my life. LOL.

It was always great to have family and visitors. It's no secret how important this is to your recovery. To have this interaction brings hope to you. It makes you feel hopeful that you will go home. It was about this time that the boy's grandparents came to visit me from out of town. It was awesome to see them both, but then you think, *Damn, I must be hurt if people are coming from out of town to see me.* Because of Covid-19, I could only have one guest at a time. It was hard to see everyone, and I realized it was exhausting to see people back to back. But you needed it so bad, like filling up your emotional gas tank.

ଓଃ

I spent a great day with my kid's grandpa. Over the years, we have created a great bond and we would always sit and talk when they would come to town and mostly laugh. I was not surprised when the first thing he said was, "Wow. I thought you would look a lot worse.

I said, "Well, I could pull one of these plugs out. Might get ugly quick." We both laughed. I had such a great visit with him.

I realized two things during that visit: it hurts to laugh when you have broken ribs and I couldn't laugh out loud. I was laughing but no sound was coming out. You start to see all of the small after effect injuries or things that happen because of an injury. You wonder which ones will heal and which ones won't.

I started to realize what my family was going through. They were dealing with my life at home. the dogs. paying my bills because they had no access to my money, coming to visit me…I know this place is far from our house. This was turning into a test for everyone, and it showed. Something like this effects everyone in your family and friends.

This was also the time my family thought I was good enough to have a cell phone. I was so excited. It was like a lifeline to my life again. My son Zack was my power of attorney so he and the family went to the cell phone store to hook up an old phone so I didn't have my new one in the hospital just in case something would happen to it. It was a good idea. I have not had any personal items on me up to this point, so I was super excited to get something of my own.

The next day Zack brought it to me at the hospital and I yelled, "Yay, my son is here," and he laughed. It was one of his mom's old phones, complete with a purple phone case, but I was glad to have it. I am not gonna lie. I cried. I could finally text people, watch videos and movies…man now I was living! LOL. There was just one problem: I realized I couldn't see right. Like, it seemed like I had double vision and could no longer see up close.

I explained to boy's mom, Mariam, what was going on. She brought me some reading glasses and it helped to read my phone, but something seemed off. Everything else hurt so I didn't worry about it.

And when I say pain, again, I was so surprised how much pain I could take. There are some things we never know until we are tested. I was getting off a lot of drugs and I was amazed at how many crazy dreams I would have. Sleeping at night was like torture. I would stay up as late as I could until I passed out. Also, the tough part of the night was the constant waking up every couple hour for blood test or check blood pressure or shots. I can say I had to get two shots in my stomach every day and it was the worst. Little did I know I would get over 100 before I would be done.

Every day I would ask everyone when they thought I would go home. They would say, "Soon. We just need to get you off all these machines and get those tubes out of you." I had five tubes coming out of my stomach with little balls on the ends that collected stuff. She said, "People drain those every day for you. Never touch them."

I asked, "How the hell is that even possible? Those thigs are connected to my insides and coming out of me. How do they get them out?"

She said, "We will leave that for another day." LOL.

I also had a trach in my neck that they had to change every day. It was no fun and being a singer, I was afraid to have that in my neck and what it would do to my voice. I had a speaking valve in so you could talk when it was in, but at night there was a lady who came by and took it out so you could only speak or yell a little bit.

After a few days, my doctor came in and said She was going to change my trach out to a different size. I had no idea what was happening. I just said, "Sure."

She said, "Lay back." She grabbed my neck and it felt like she was strangling me. I could feel something coming out of my neck. It was so weird.

She said, "You're done."

I was like *What the hell just happened?* This lady was one of the good ones. She helped me in a lot of ways. You can tell the ones that are in your corner rooting for you are good people.

You must do whatever they say in order to get better, go through whatever it takes to get out of here. Remember, I slept through my first month, and five major surgeries. I thought the tough stuff was behind me, but it seems like I'm in for the long haul now. Each thing or procedure I had to go through would be just another piece of the puzzle of putting me back together again. I am feeling better, and my mind feels like it's pretty good, but I still can't move out of my bed. I tried but I got so dizzy, I started to feel like a prisoner in my body. I wanted to move. My mind was telling me to get up, but I couldn't do it. I could only lay there, and I was moving legs and arms but felt like my body was so broken.

It makes you humble for sure. Each day, now, there are lots of tests and they are trying to get rid of things you don't need and graduate you to the next level of care. It sounded good until my nurse came in one day and I was laying there.

She said, "I just need to check something."

I said, "Cool." She was very chatty, and I was talking back to her and felt her reach under my gown to my private area. I thought, *Finally a nurse who gets me! LOL.*

Then I felt a yank and extreme pain and I said, "What are you doing?" At this point, she knew I was onto her, so she just pulled. Out came a catheter. I swear I saw Jesus at that moment! LOL.

I said, "What was that?"

She said, "This was in your pee-pee. Now you're going to go like a big boy," and laughed.

I said, "That was the worst pain I ever felt! Damn!"

She said, "Believe it or not, you'll thank me later."

She was right.

Man, everything from brain scans at two in the morning to x-rays and blood tests…this was a tough month for me, but I knew I was getting better now. I could feel my body parts reconnecting to the mother board and my mind starting to fire on all cylinders.

When I see my doctors now, they always say, "How's "The Miracle"?"

I say, "Great man. Feeling better. What happens next? I want to go home."

They kept saying. "We can't believe how quickly you are healing. It's amazing."

I said, "Well, I thought I hired the best. LOL."

They would say to me, "You have the best sense of humor. We think it has a big impact on your recovery."

CHAPTER FOUR

TIP #3: A SENSE OF HUMOR

Have a great sense of humor. At this point, the damage is done. There is only getting through recovery. I found that when I joked and laughed, it made me feel better and more normal. Plus, think of these poor health care workers battling through a pandemic, working their ass off at a thankless job. How cool is it to work with a guy who almost died and is a mess, but he is making you laugh? It's like paying them back for caring for you and they want to see you again and are glad to help you. I laughed and cried with a lot of my nurses. They're angels.

The key is you can't think, "Oh poor me," or "Why me?" and get all negative about your situation. I know it's hard, but you lived, so hit the reset button and let's go. Is it gonna be easy? No, no it's not, but you can do it because I did, and I never thought I would make it. Manage your expectations to reduce disappointments. The roller coaster you are on has left the station. You will have great days and bad days. Hang in there. You got this, so laugh a little.

So, like I said earlier, lots of doctors come see me throughout the day. During a visit with one of my surgeons, he said, "Man you're doing amazing. Soon you'll be off to rehab to get better."

I said, "What do you mean? I have to go somewhere else before I go home?"

He said, "Yeah, man. We get you better and off all the machines, then you go to a rehabilitation center to learn how to walk and talk and how to take care of yourself again." I couldn't believe what I was hearing. I just got really quiet, and he said, "You'll do great, man. You'll be home soon."

I called the boys mom, Mariam, and asked her to visit me as soon as she could. The next day was Saturday, and she came to visit. Keep in mind, this is one of the few people I trust to give it to me straight. She was amazing at getting me through this tough process.

She said, "Listen, this is a long process. Number one, they saved your life. Number two, they're getting you off all the lifesaving equipment and machines. And number three, you will have to learn how to walk and talk and take care of yourself."

I said, "I can't do that."

She said, "You don't have a choice."

I laughed and thought, *Damn, she always wins. LOL. How did I end up here?*

She said, "That guy really nailed you. It will take at least a year before you're better."

I said, "Man, it's been like five months already."

She said, "No, it's only been six weeks."

I laugh as I write this because I had a horrible sense of time through this whole thing, even now. LOL. This was really tough news for me to hear and hard to process that I couldn't do the things she said. It was hard to take that I wasn't going home anytime soon.

ꕤ

As I laid there, I thought, *Man, the irony. I never drank alcohol my whole life then I almost get killed by a drunk driver. What a bitch!* It rang in my head.

She said, "You were a victim of a crime."

I never thought about it that way. I started to think about this guy. Who is he? What is his story? And who the fuck is driving drunk at 10:30 on a Sunday morning? I knew that I could hate this guy and spend a ton of bad energy thinking about what I could do to him or what will happen to him. But I knew that I lived and that was not the lesson I needed to learn. I needed to forgive him in my mind so I could wash away the negativity from this event. I knew I was so broken physically that there was no way I could drag that negative energy with me through my recovery.

My mental sharpness would have to be at the top of its game in order to heal fast and get back to my new normal. Forgiveness is a gift you give yourself. It's not really for the other person. They just become the recipient of your new positive energy. Every time I would tell someone my story, they would ask, "Did they get the guy that did that?"

I said, "Yeah, I forgive him. He will pay his own price. Life will give us both the lessons we were supposed to learn through this event." Still sucks to be me though. LOL. But I know that he has kids and is a dad, so this will affect his family, too. His kids will also be without their dad for a long time. So many lives changed with one bad decision.

Now I have added forgiveness to my toolbox, and I understand the difference between forgiving something and completely releasing myself from that thing, so it has no power in my thoughts. I think this is ultimately the type of lessons we are meant to explore along the way.

CHAPTER FIVE: STARTING OVER

Over the next couple days, I find I am feeling better. I hear the doctors start to say, "I think there's not a lot more we can do for you here. Make sure you arrange your rehabilitation so we can start to get you out of here." It was like a shot of adrenaline. I finally had something to look forward to.

The next day, my nurse informed me that I would have to complete a few simple tasks before they could release me, and we would be working on those this week. I have to admit, when she mentioned a few, like sit in a wheelchair, chew crushed up food, pee in a bottle thing, LOL, I thought, *I've been training all my life for this moment. I got this*. LOL.

I didn't have it, not even close.

That week was very tough. I was amazed at how I couldn't do the simplest things, Day one was a disaster. They put me in a chair. I was supposed to sit in it for an hour. I couldn't believe the pain. This was first time I was in a position other than lying flat on my back.

Everything that I didn't know hurt because I was on my back was now killing me. I am in this chair, broken neck, broken hips, broken ribs. I'm so dizzy I can barely hold my head straight; I am thinking, *God I would like to change my answer. I'm done*. There were a few moments during this journey that I was face to face with how badly I was hurt. This day was one of them. So, after about 10 minutes, I said, "Please put me back in bed."

They said, "You can do it. Hang in there."

I said, "Not today."

It was crushing.

That night, after crying myself to sleep, I had a "come to Jesus" moment. I knew that if I wanted to go home, I would have to reduce the pain somehow to reach my goals. I have done self-hypnosis in the past and knew it could help me during my recovery. So, the next day they sat me up in the chair and, again, extreme pain. I said, "Just leave me alone a second," and after a couple of deep breaths, I got into the zone. I imagined I was on a hot sunny beach in Hawaii, and I just kept focusing on the sun on my face and how hot it was. I made it 20 minutes. It felt like I had a plan and was working better, but there was still a lot of pain. But I was getting off all the machines. It was time to eat and drink on my own.

I have not taken a drink of water in over six weeks so when the nurse came in with a big glass of ice water, I stared at it for a good minute then took the straw in my mouth. I took a small sip. It was so cold, so good, and a big day for me. I couldn't believe it. I took another.

She said, "Slow down. I know, it's great right?"

Wow! For the first time to drink on my own, it was like a new independence. Later that day she came back with a Sprite for me to taste. I took a sip, and it was amazing. I think I cried; it was so good. It was like tasting it for the first time. I also realized that something was up with my tongue and my taste buds. Before she left, she said, "I'll be back tomorrow. In order to leave, you have to be able to eat some food on your own." Sounded simple but I am a very picky eater, and I was not sure how this would go down.

Meanwhile back at the ranch, Mariam had picked a rehab place for me to go to. It was close to the house so it would be easier for everyone to visit me. It sounded good to me. I just wanted to get out of there. And now, we are six weeks into my family getting my dogs every day, taking them to their house then bringing them home at night. They were amazing. Everyone had their task and shift. I was so proud that they came to my rescue.

Towards the end of the week, I started seeing tons of doctors, getting tons of scans, x-rays, blood tests… I could tell they were making sure I was ready for my next level of care. Finally, I see my main doctor. He said, “Man, you really are “The Miracle.” I’m so proud of all the work you put in, so I am getting you out of here on Friday by the end of the day.” I couldn’t believe I survived to this point, and I would be leaving. I really thought I would die here. It was a great new reality.

I had to be cleared by my neck and brain surgeon. She was a super serious, sharp lady. When she came in, I was nervous about the results of my scans the night before. She’s always so serious, it was hard to read her. She said, “I had another doctor look at your brain scan.”

And I said, “Did you find one?”

She smiled slightly and said, “You had a small amount of bleeding on your brain from the accident which has cleared up completely and your neck is healing great. You no longer need your neck brace.” I just cried. I was so happy. She gave me a nice hug and said, “Come see me when you get better.”

So, now it was down to eating for someone and I could get out of there.

It was Friday. I was supposed to leave today, if all goes well. Everyone who comes in my room is so excited for me. They gave me a bath, washing my hair… it was like prom night, baby! LOL. They said transportation would be there to get me at the end of the day. It was then I found out that I would travel by ambulance to my new rehabilitation center in Peoria.

I also thought the trach in my neck would come out as planned, but they said they couldn't get orders to do it so the next place would do it for me. I am not going to lie. I was excited but also scared to death. I had no idea where I was going and what that place might be like. I knew I did not have a good experience here, and even though they saved my life and there are tons of amazing caring people that helped me, there were a couple that made it tough being there.

Finally, at the end of the day, my food shows up. The lady says, "Sorry. I could only get a plate of broccoli salad and a drink."

I said, "I hate that shit. I can't eat that. I mean, that's my first meal. What the fuck?"

She said, "You just need to take a bite so I can say I saw you eat, and swallow then drink."

I said, "Okay, I get it."

I took a bit in my mouth then pointed at my drink. When she turned around to get it, I quickly spat the food into my hand and then dropped it onto the floor. She handed me the drink. I took a drink and said, "We cool?"

She said, "Yeah, that's what I needed."

Now it was official. I was heading out. They were getting my paperwork together and all the nurses were stopping in saying goodbye and wishing me luck. It was hard. These people worked so hard to get me to this point. Big hugs for everyone. Now, it was a waiting game for transportation to come get me. It was around 5:00 p.m. when they finally came. I was exhausted by then. They rolled the gurney into my room and said, "Pick up for Jay Neyens."

I was like, "I called an Uber." They laughed and started to load me up. It took a good half hour to get the paperwork and make sure they had everything, and then we started down the hall.

There were people on both sides of the hall clapping and shaking my hands. It felt great. We got downstairs and rolled outside, and I said, "Damn, I haven't been in the sun in a long time. It feels so good."

The dude was like, "Let me let you sit here while I do something."

Before they loaded me up, he sat me in the sun so I could soak up some sunshine while he made a phone call or something, but I knew he just wanted me to get to feel the sun on my face for a second. It felt so amazing.

They loaded me in and locked me down and we hit the road. The guy in the back was super nice and chatty, so I didn't think about that fact I was driving until she hit the brakes. I grabbed the side of the gurney.

Dude says, "You okay?"

I said, "First ride."

He said, "Oh, I get it. Well, we're 45 minutes out. Just get some rest."

My mind was racing. I had no idea where I was going or what would be next. I have never been anywhere like this, so I wasn't sure what to expect.

It was about 7:30 p.m. or so by the time we made it to the rehabilitation center on the west side of Peoria. The sun was just setting. It was so beautiful. Again, as they took me out, the guy said, "Maybe you should sit and watch this for a second.:

I said, "Dude, you're the man. Thanks." Again, at each part of my journey there are these amazing people who take just a second to make things a little better.

Because the ride was so far, I thought it was really far away from my house. I did not really know where I was, and I thought I was in the wrong place, I think, but here I was. As they rolled me in, there was a lot of construction going on and I saw a lot of older people. It seemed more like a retirement home, so I started to freak out a bit. I thought, *Maybe I'm not going home. This sucks.*

I stopped the guy and said, "Dude are we in the right place?"

He said, "Yeah, man. This is where they told us to bring you." So, we rolled to the end of the hall were a guy and a lady were standing, and they said, "Jay Neyens."

I thought, *Oh they know where I am.*

I am rolled into a room where they put me on a table, get me naked and start to take pictures. I was like, "Man, things don't usually progress this fast. LOL."

She said, "We need to document what shape you're in when you get here.

I am like, "Okay, that works."

By now it's night and the vibe is always weird at night. I am not sure why, but I started to get nervous. They moved me into my room, #112, the last one on the end next to another wing under construction. Once I was there, I said, "Could I get some water and something to eat?"

She said, "Your chart says no water or food."

I was like, "No. I just started to eat and drink a couple days ago so please I am really thirsty."

She again said, "Sorry. I can only do what's on the chart."

I said, "But if I don't have a feeding tube and no IV for fluids, how do I eat or drink?" Now it's really late. I call the boy's mom about midnight. She's a trooper. She called the old hospital and found out that they forgot to send my updated status paperwork and they would fax it over right away. I was not happy. I was screaming over phone, "Get me out of here, please. I need new place."

She said, "Just give it a chance. We will talk in the morning."

Then a nurse appeared in my room with drinks and crackers. She said, "I'm so sorry. We got your new orders and you're all set now."

I said, "Good."

She said, "Can I say something?"

I said, "Sure."

She said, "Remember your first day of school every year? It's scary, all new people and new place but give us a chance. You'll be fine." She grabbed my hand, squeezed it then walked out.

I thought, *Damn, I hate when that happens*, but she was right. It put me at ease, so I fell asleep. What a day I had but here I was hopefully entering the final stretch before I went home. I was woken up early the next day. Guess I have a roommate. He was up early, and I hear him coughing a lot. The nurses went to his side a lot. I guess he was recovering from Covid, someone said. So, I put on my mask. I wasn't sure how long he had it but turns out he was at the same hospital I was, and he also just got there a couple days earlier.

The floor nurse shows up to give me my meds and tell me how everything works. She was an awesome, funny, happy, caring lady who called everyone "Boo." I was so relived after talking with her and I knew I could give it a go. There were tons of CNAs coming in and out asking if I needed anything and it seemed like a lot of hustle and bustle going on.

Again, so many people taking my vitals, and my blood pressure every couple of hours. No food yet but now they know I am here. You get to order your food the day before, breakfast, lunch and dinner. This was about to be a problem because I am so picky but turns out they have an extra page which had everything I needed to make it. LOL.

The boy's mom called and asked if I was ok and if I would give it a try there. I said yes. She was happy to avoid another situation. I spent the day just lying in bed. I spoke a bit to my roommate and just tried to get use to my new environment. I was beat so I took a nap. Even during your nap, they are taking vitals and, of course, my shots twice a day in the stomach. Man, I hate those.

As night closed in, I noticed there was a shift change around 6:00 p.m. and my floor nurse came in and said, "Okay, Boo, I am leaving. This is what's up for you tomorrow." I felt great that there was a game plan. As the night rolled on, there was constant care every couple of hours, and something was always going on. I had my nightly calls from family. Mariam would always check in to make sure I was good and see if I needed anything, and then the boy's grandpa would call to usually make me laugh and cheer me up a bit.

This is something he did through my whole time in recovery and after. Everyone, these are the simple things you can do for someone that makes a huge difference in that person's recovery. Please, reach out to someone who needs it. When I spoke with Mariam, she asked, "So, can you make it at this place?"

I said, "Yeah. I think it's going to be ok."

CHAPTER SIX

I felt so blessed to hear from so many people from all phases of my life, reaching out, showing support. Shout to my old school friend from back home. He would message me every week and check in on me on Facebook. It motivated me to win this battle for everyone.

About 8:00 p.m., every night, the nurse comes in with my meds. I don't know what they are but it's a handful and I don't like to take pills. I have to take a big drink and throw my head back which worked out perfect with a broken neck. LOL. But it became entertainment when new CNAs would come to watch me take my pills. It looked more like a seizure then a pill drop but I made it work. LOL.

Night is painful. It's when my body is hard at work trying to recover. Every night before I fell asleep, I would body scan to determine which part of my body has the most pain and concentrate on that area, trying to send all the positive energy to that area to heal. I know this sounds crazy, but it seemed to help me heal faster and get in touch with my body as I continued to learn all the things that happened to me.

I realized that every night it would be hard to sleep as I would hear my roommate try to breath. Covid-19 is a wicked virus. At first, for so many nights, I thought it would be his last. Thank God he recovered.

After just a couple hours of sleep, I was woken by a familiar face. It was the girl who told me to hang in there, that this was the first day of school. She said, "Glad to see you stayed."

I said, "Well, I have a couple more weeks of school, so I am going to stick it out. LOL."

The days around here start early with another shift change again about 6:00 a.m., it seems like, so I am up watching a little TV, watching the news like I did every morning to help me catch up. I felt so out of sync with the outside world. Breakfast arrived, bacon, eggs, toast, fruit cup… ok I am in. I was still really new at eating on my own, but I took it slow and easy. I didn't want them to think I couldn't do it. I made some small talk with my roommate and we're not sure what's next for our day. Then in walks what looks like another young nurse or doctor, not sure, but she seemed very confident. She said, "Hi, I am Hannah."

I said, "I love that name. That's my niece's name."

She said, "Cool. Then you'll remember me." She asked, "So, how mobile are you? Have you been doing therapy at the other hospital?"

I said, "Just a little but I can't really get out of bed or anything."

She laughed and said, "Well, we're gonna change that."

After a poor attempt at sitting up and doing some basic exercise in my bed so she could evaluate my mobility, she said, "Looks like you have some work to do."

I said, "I am ready. I am just so broken."

She looked me right in the eye, seemed like my soul, and said, "You can do this, Jay. We just have to start from the beginning."

It was weird. Those words weighed so heavy on me. It sounded so hard to accomplish from where I was, but she said it with such confidence, almost like she knew what my outcome would be. Somehow, I trusted this one like a guardian angel. I couldn't explain it. Sometimes people are placed in your life for a reason, and I knew if I did what she said, I would get my reward.

This process was tough, to constantly hand over your humility to strangers in order to regain your humanity, but these people are the helpers, the heroes. This is how it works.

Hannah was a tough, by the book kind of girl, very sweet but if you think she's not counting those leg lifts, you're wrong. LOL. I am not much for rules. I pretty much sailed my own ship my whole life so I would have to make amends with this one for sure. LOL.

She said, "Okay, see you tomorrow.

I said, "How many days a week is therapy?"

She said, "Every day at 7:00."

I thought, *Well here we go. It's now or never.* It was at that moment I committed myself to walking out of that rehab center, not with a wheelchair or a walker. I was walking out on my own two feet. She didn't know it, but I would make her proud. Meanwhile, I could barely sit up on my own to grab the remote, LOL, but I got this.

She also said, "Have your family bring you some normal clothes to wear, like sweats or whatever you want."

I said, "No shit, really?"

She said, "Yeah, you don't have to look like a patient. Whatever makes you feel normal." I sent a text to Mariam as soon as she left the room.

This really was a game changer, a huge psychological win for me. If I can dress normal, I can feel normal. If I don't look like a patient maybe I won't feel like one. So now, I got a phone, a drawer to put stuff in and a bed to sleep in, TV to watch, three hot meals a day… I might be good.

Side note: I remember telling my son Zack that I was having a lot of bad dreams when I was at the big hospital. I said, "Like crazy stuff, things trying to kill me and eat me." He laughed and I said, "What's funny about that? LOL."

He said, "When you were in a coma at the first hospital, every time I came in to see you they had your TV on the Discovery Channel hoping it would stimulate you. But it was shark week. LOL. So, I finally asked them to change it to something

more soothing. Guess you were listening after all."

ஐ

It's lunch time. I realized being at the end of the hall was first food delivery and they bring you what you order the day before or close to it. I realized that all my food was in small pieces. I guess I need to take a test to have big boy food but at this point, I'll take anything. With lunch is a soda and dessert, so I thought, *This food thing is going to work out for me*. I was weighing in at like 128 pounds, down from 164 a couple of months earlier. A good wind could take me out. I had no muscle and very little mobility. This was a tough place to start from, but I knew if I was positive and joked around and lived in the moment, I could do it.

It was about this time I also realized that I couldn't see very good. It was like double vision or something. I had thought something was up at the last hospital but there were so many things wrong, and I didn't have my glasses, so I wasn't sure. But now I am. If I close one eye, I see fine. "Then just close the other eye, I can see great. Open both eyes and "Houston, we have a problem."

I text Mariam and ask her to bring my glasses to see if that would help. They were making a list of stuff to bring me. It felt more like I am moving in for the long haul so I was getting a little worried about how long I might be there. Later I would find out that my eyes might be my biggest hurdle to overcome.

After lunch, it's nap time. It takes so much energy just to sit up, eat, talk a little to my roommate... it seems like we have a lot in common, so it gives us a lot to bullshit about during day.

You just crash. You can't help it. Your body shuts down so you can rest and heal. Your body does what it needs to heal, like being on auto pilot. I am here and want to help but my body is still in control. It's a weird feeling. Your body lets you wake up to nourish it but only gives you moments in time for the real world then it's back out. But it never fails. A couple hours into a good nap and somebody is poking your ass or taking vitals or something. LOL. But it's all good.

It's almost dinner time which comes fast it seems. Nice chicken dinner with mashed potatoes, like comfort food. Man, just what I needed. I am still only a couple days into eating and my body is craving food. When it's time to eat, I am like a dog at the end of the leash. And again, I am super picky, but I am not kicking anything to the side of the plate. However, I notice that I don't taste things the same, but I am not sure what that is. I'll think about it later. Right now, I just eat.

CHAPTER SEVEN

As an artist, some of the best therapy I get is in my studio creating art. I thought it would be cool to do a series of Spirit Animals that helped me make it through my recovery. I used a mixed media method, and they represent each animal in its spirit form.

THE SPIRIT WOLF

The WOLF in the spirit world represents instinct, intelligence and the need for freedom.

For this part of my journey, the wolf represented the call to action. I had to trust that there was a team of amazing doctors and nurses and specialist that would not only communicate with my family and friends, but also save my life and put me back together again. This is the first phase of what would be a long hard struggle. I was in and out of a coma for most of this phase so, as a pack animal, I had to count on my pack to do everything they needed to help me survive.

The Miracle

THE KING

In the spirit world. The LION represents the relentless fighter as well as courage, strength and strategy.

This spirit animal is what represented my second phase: recovery.

This was the point in my recovery when I was starting to understand what had happen to me and I realized the fight I would have ahead of me. I understood I almost died in a very bad car accident, and it would take all of my courage to endure the pain it would take to get better. I knew I would have to have the strength of the lion to help me through months of physical therapy and medical procedures.

I was so broken. I knew this would be the fight of my life.

THE MIRACLE

THE STALLION

In the spirit world, the HORSE represents passion, drive and an appetite for freedom and strong emotions.

This was the perfect spirit animal for the 3rd phase of my recovery, I just moved to my new rehabilitation center and was about to learn how to walk, talk and brush my teeth again. This is where I would meet the person who would change my life. She gave me the passion to get better. My appetite for freedom was real. I asked every day when I was going home. This was also a time of growing, relearning, understanding and very, very strong emotions.

The Miracle

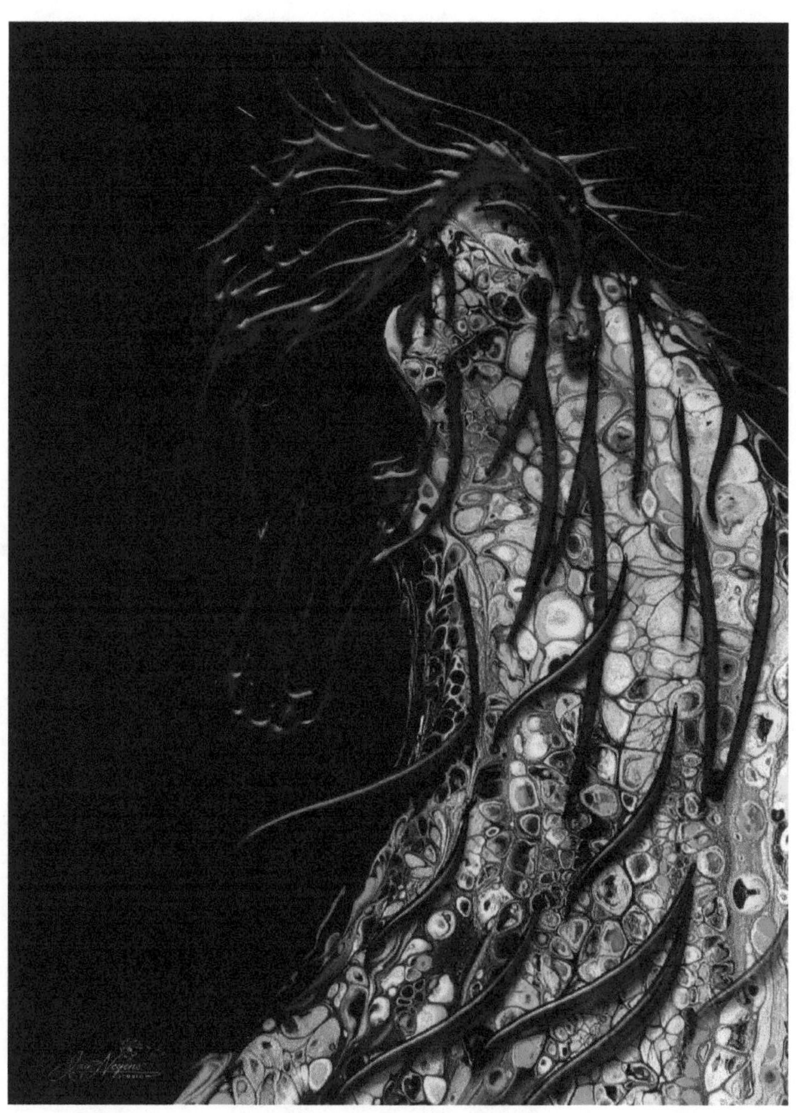

THE SPIRIT OWL

In the spirit world, the OWL represents intuition, wisdom and change. The owl can see what others can't see.

I think the owl is great to represent the fourth phase of my recovery. By this point, I am going home, and I would have to use all of my new knowledge and wisdom to keep myself safe yet continue to recover. I would have to embrace all the new changes that would make up my new normal.

And, at this point, I realize that my intuition has not only changed but has become a new gift in my journey of recovery.

The Miracle

THE PHOENIX

The PHOENIX represents rebirth, change, new beginnings.

I put in the work, I endured the pain, but best of all, I beat the odds. Now it's time to become the new me and transform into the new normal. Time to stop thinking of myself as a victim and see myself as a survivor.

Time to start thinking about what I can do, not the things I can't do. This year has changed my life forever. I know I not the same person. I have lost the ability to do some things but yet I gained the ability to do things I couldn't do before. I still have a long recovery ahead of me but the new me has it under control.

You too can rise from the ashes.

The Miracle

CHAPTER EIGHT

It's about 6:00 and, again, I notice a shift change. My floor nurse always seems to come and say goodbye, which is cool. Three times a day, my respiratory therapist nurse comes in and changes my trach. I am always a big boy about it, but I hate it.

And again, I think anybody that has been in a hospital, or these rehabilitation centers, would agree that nighttime is much different then daytime. I'm not really sure why, but I never like the night. I think part of it is I still have nightmares every night and its never dark or quiet. I'm close to a nurse's station and it's a gathering spot at night. I must admit, I did like just watching a little TV at night, trying to relax and prepare my mind for the next day. After my nightly meds, I am out, but it's not long before I am up at 1:00 in the morning for chest x-rays then back to sleep until next vitals check.

But always around 4:00am my neck will wake me up to let me know it's still broken. Plus, it's freezing in our room. The AC is cranking all the time, so I have five blankets over me trying not to freeze. This is when I missed sleeping with my two dogs, Jett and Willow. Jett is like a big bear; I could have used him then. LOL.

I think about the dogs a lot. They are Australian Shepherds. They are very smart, and I am sure they are wondering what happened to the old man. He said he would be right back. LOL. But again, this shows how these tragedies affect everyone. They bark at me on the phone when I call the boys, so I assume they know I am somewhere. The boys send pics, and these are the things that help your recovery.

I am awake early, watching TV, wondering what today will hold and, like clockwork, in walks Hannah. She says, "Hi guys," opens the curtains to let in the sun, opens the curtains between my roommate and me, and starts cleaning up a bit. There was a white board in our room and every day, they would put who was on shift and what our limitations were. Mine said "Non weight bearing, left side and neck brace when up."

My weight bearing status would not change until they day before I was released due to my broken hip.

Once she had our ship in order, she said, "Are you ready?"

I said, "Okay. Let's do it."

We did some bed exercises and then she said, "Do you think you can stand up?"

I said, "Not sure. I haven't done that before."

She said, "Okay, well first sit up." LOL.

I did that and, man, I got so dizzy! She taught me how to look across the room at something and focus, then it would go away. But damn! That was bad.

I scooted to the end of the bed. She pulled my walker in front of me then basically put a strap around both of us and said, "1… 2… 3… up," and she pulled, and I stood up. I couldn't believe it. I was standing. I could feel the blood rushing to my feet. It was weird. I didn't feel strong, but she had me and I trusted this one. I just enjoyed that moment and thought, *Damn, I can do this*. Now remember, I am bearing all my weight on one leg because she would not let me put any weight on my bad leg. But I did it. I stood up. That was huge for me. I am sure I cried but I cried a lot at that point. There was very little control over my emotions; that's the head injury talking.

But it felt like my sensation had been locked up in my body somewhere and then, when I stood up, I could feel the sensation running down into the lower part of my body. It was like everything just got plugged back in.

So, she brought in a wheelchair and said, "This is yours. It will be in your room to get around so let's learn how to get in and out of it."

I thought, *Man, a new level of freedom. If I can get in and out of this thing, I can be mobile, maybe sneak out the back door. LOL.* Turns out, I would chase my mobility for the next year or more.

But I was up for it. I tried the best I could to get in and out, but tired quickly. Hannah would always support me and say something about using all my spoons up before the day is over. I didn't know what the hell she was talking about but later it would be a valuable lesson that she taught me.

I ate some lunch and was ready to crash. After my nap, I made my phone calls to share the news with my family that I had stood up for the first time and was very happy about my progress.

It's almost like I just needed to stand that one time and I knew I would walk again for sure. That night before bed, I did self-hypnosis and just got into the zone and told my mind that tonight we needed to work on my legs. I needed to feel strength again. I needed to feel sturdy like a huge oak tree. I needed to feel the blood flow again and told my workman to go to work. When I woke up the next day, I felt great. It was like my legs felt different in a good way but there was one 8-inch round spot on my upper leg above the knee that was totally numb. This was freaking me out a bit. I knew I had a spinal cord injury and a bad ass surgeon who helped me to walk again, but I didn't know what was going on.

When Hannah came in for my morning therapy, she said, "What's up?"

I said, "I feel good, but there's this one spot on my leg that is numb."

She said, "It's okay. All of your nerves were put on notice yesterday that you might want to walk again, so your body is reconnecting and adjusting from sitting in bed for so long. But mention it to your doctors when they come in."

It made sense and it felt good to hear it from her. I trusted Hannah. There were always so many different people coming in and out, but this was the first consistent person that showed up every day from my recovery team.

It's amazing, really, that there was such a large team of people connected to my journey. Every day it seemed a new doctor or nurse would walk in and tell me something new that happened to me.

One doctor came in and said, "I hear you're absent of a spleen."

I said, "I don't know. I haven't seen it. Do I need it?"

He said, "It's helpful, but you can live without it."

I thought, *Great. What next?*

And remember, there are so many people that touch you in such a short amount of time to save your life, it's very hard later to figure out who did what, but I'm glad they did whatever it took to save me.

My son dropped off some clothes for me today. I couldn't wait. Not only did I love to see him, but I would love to dress normal tomorrow. He called me from my house. They were going through my closet, showing me clothes to pick out. It was like shopping again but from my closet. LOL.

Again, Zack had really been hands on during my recovery. He visited me every time he could and took care of all my business stuff and ran errands. I love that kid. My son Josh was still having trouble visiting me, which I totally understand. But he supported me any way he could. They are both very strong young men, and this has been crazy tough on all of us.

So, seeing Zack took my mood from a four to a 10. I was so happy. He brought me a bunch of clothes and a bunch of junk food. I was in heaven. What a guy! My family always took care of me.

After Zack left, I had a great chicken dinner and chatted again with my roommate as we surfed the channels looking for something to watch. We liked the same music, so we had a lot of life in common.

More meds and shots, and it was off to sleep.

CHAPTER NINE

The next day I woke up early and I was ready to go. I had one of the CNAs help me get dressed for the first time. It was hard, but I did it. Only socks; still no shoes yet. She also got me my own kit to shave and brush my teeth, comb my hair… it was like a big boy kit. But it meant I was getting better, and I could master these few things that I have done for years but now couldn't do to save my life. LOL.

She said, "Try to comb your hair."

I was like, "No problem," and I grab the comb, but it was like, *What is happening?* I got it to my head, but not sure if I was combing it or rubbing it on my head. I laughed and said, "My son will bring me a hat." LOL.

I was so surprised how the most basic things were so difficult to do, but I knew the only way out of here was to be able to take care of myself. I rubbed my head all day with that damn comb until it looked like I brushed it. When Hannah showed up, I looked ready to go.

She was like, "Okay. You look more normal. How does that make you feel?"

I said, "Great. Like I'm better and I'm just waiting for the bus to pick me up." LOL

We did our normal warmups and then worked on getting in and out of my wheelchair. It was hard to sit with my broken hip, but I wanted to get mobile. She put a big pillow on the seat and seemed to work, making it easier to sit. I was still so dizzy getting up and down, but she said it would go away as time goes on. She had an answer for everything. LOL.

After lunch that day, I noticed that my roommate would also have a therapy session in the afternoon with Occupational Therapy. I did not have that yet and wasn't sure if I would. Different stroke for different folks, but it looked hard, so I was hoping he was on a different program.

So, I asked Hannah when I would get out of here and she said, "I think, if all goes well, maybe around Thanksgiving."

This was around September 28th, and I couldn't believe what she was saying. I was devastated. It seemed like forever. I was trying to keep my composure but damn.

She said, "Listen. This is a long road. You have a lot of injuries, and you still have all these tubes sticking out of you, bones that need to heal… Be patient. You'll get there."

It feels nice to have friends on your side to talk you down from the cliff when you need it. I spoke with the boy's mom that night and she said the same thing. "Listen to me. The boys have got your life on auto pilot at the moment. Your bills are all paid, and you just need to focus on your recovery. Don't worry about anything else right now."

At that point, I surrendered a bit, I guess. I laid there and thought, *Okay, constant 24-hour care, three great meals a day, TV to watch, I am getting more mobile. Some chick is teaching me to walk again. Okay this will have to work, I guess*. Did I mention there is a snack cart with tons of junk food on it? Mental note: get Zack to bring me some cash. I need to get set up with a snack budget.

This was my reality now. Even though I was getting better, I was weeks from going home. But I did want to be home for the holidays, and anything could still go wrong. I know I have to be released by several doctors so I'm starting to wonder how all that works and who arranges all that.

Many doctors continued to stream through my room and I aways answer them, give them my concerns, but mostly they just say, "You're looking great. Keep working." But I'm a firm believer that the more normal I look and act, the better I will feel. Transform from a patient to a person just recovering. I remember it was a couple weeks after Hannah had me up and mobile that I was fully dressed and sitting in my wheelchair scrolling through my phone when a doctor I haven't seen yet walked in and said, "Oh sorry. I was looking for Jay Neyens."

I said, "Yeah, that's me."

He was really quiet and looked down at his chart that showed all my injuries before he slowly looked back up and said, "You're the guy with all these injuries?"

I said, "I guess so. No one lets me read the list." LOL.

He said, "Man, you're The Miracle! You look amazing."

I said, "Well, I'm not going to lie. I have shit to do and people to see so I want to get out of here." LOL.

He said, "Can I look at your tubes?"

I said, "Sure." I laid on my bed, opened my shirt and there was a wrap on me around my body like a girdle. He had my floor nurse, Boo, cut it off of me and there were five tubes sticking out of my body with bottles on the ends collecting fluids.

I said, "What are they?"

He said, "They're connected to parts of you inside and draining fluids. The nurse empties them every morning. Once they stop draining, I will take them out."

I said, "How do they do that?"

He said, "We just pull them out." LOL.

What? How is it even possible to have tubes sticking out of you like that? My poor stomach looked like a warzone with a 12-inch scar down the middle and these tubes. It was crazy. And now, I have nothing to hold them down, so the tubes are hanging everywhere, and the drainage balls are in the pockets of my sweatpants. This makes everything harder, but I hoped to get them out soon.

I do think I was able to recover quicker because I didn't know the full extent of my injuries. I think I would have been afraid to move, and it would have been overwhelming. Better to ease me into my new reality. The better I got mentally, the better I could handle new information. I remember the boys' grandpa would always say stay positive and just adjust to the new information. Sounded easy enough. LOL.

Over the next couple of weeks, I would get a lot of new information and I also started to understand that I would have to take on a few more responsibilities in order to put the pieces of my life back together.

But it was Friday, and I made it through my first week. I was excited to see my family and my buddy George over the weekend. I had so much to talk with them about and I would be able to show them a few new tricks Hannah showed me. There were COVID restriction in place so only one person at a time could visit which made it tough, but better than nothing.

Friday night was a great meal and my roommate, and I watched some TV and listened to tunes. I was feeling great about this place. I just didn't want to stay so long but whatever it takes. The next morning, I was up and ready and up, but no Hannah. She gave me my homework. This was the test. Would I do it without her if I could? I knew I would set up a habit that could make this recovery faster than I thought.

ଅଓ

TIP #5: FORM HABITS

Make therapy and exercise a habit. If you can do it on your own, your body will crave it and you will keep working hard whether someone is watching you or not. I wanted to do this because I knew I would be home at some point and there would be only me to hold myself accountable. If it was already a habit when I got home, it would be easier to maintain.

CHAPTER TEN

I did the best I could to get ready and someone helped me get dressed and in my wheelchair. When Mariam came in the room I stood up and gave her a hug. The look on her face was priceless. She so was happy and said, "Look at you." Keep in mind the struggle they have been through. From the beginning, she was there when I couldn't move my parts and they were not sure how bad my spinal injury was, and Zack signed off on a surgery that might help. I could see she was very hopeful that maybe I was going to walk again. Their great decisions and patience were starting to pay off. I knew it would be tough to learn to walk on one leg but that's where I had to start.

Hannah would help me up to my walker then stand behind me and hold the belt she put around me. She said, "Can you hop one step using your arms? Go for it."

I thought, *I can't walk so now I should hop??* But I did and it felt like walking. It was great. Each time I reached a goal like this, I knew that was the least I could do. Last week I could get out of bed, now I can stand up and hop. Each week I was seeing great progress. You need this to refill your soul. It takes each small win to reach the big ones and now I knew it was all about strength and endurance.

I did the homework Hannah gave me twice a day and, finally one afternoon, a girl from Occupational Therapy came in and said, "So you're Jay."

I said, "Yes ma'am." I could tell she was a sweet person.

She said, "I'm April. I'm going to work with you in the afternoons on some different things than Hannah does to get you mobile again."

I was all in but by the afternoon, I was tired and sore from the morning therapy. But she would work me for a while then put heating pads on me at the end. It was the best. Up to this point I have had mostly negative or painful interactions and to sit for a while, wrapped in heat, felt amazing. Now, I looked forward to my afternoons with her.

ᘛᘚ

I knew part of my success would require me to keep a routine the best I could. I knew when the meals came so I scheduled everything around that. When I had therapy. When I took naps. When I went to the bathroom. A schedule gave me purpose, goals and deadlines. This was finally my own structure and it felt good to have some control again.

You give up your humility to get back your humanity and now I was starting to feel just a bit more independent. I also finally took my first shower in weeks. One of the CNAs, a young kid about 22 years old, sharp, a great guy and super helpful, brought in this chair made of PVC pipe. You sit in it, and he wheels you into a shower stall, gives you some body soap and says, "Have at it."

I must have sat there in the hot water for a while. It was amazing to feel the heat and feel clean. My hair needed that. I really couldn't wash my hair great with one hand, but I didn't care. By the way, these are all the things you take for granted every day and when they are taken away, it's life changing. It was so nice to feel myself getting better and doing normal things.

Today was Saturday and my buddy George was coming to see me. This guy and his wife, Pauley, were there for my family and I couldn't wait to show him all the cool tricks Hannah taught me to do.

The last time he saw me, I was in rough shape but now I am in a new place, and I was dressed in normal clothes, just sitting in my chair when he came in. I stood up and gave him a hug. He was amazed. He was like, "OMG! Buddy, this is a miracle!"

Now, George and I go back a long time. I met him in LA. We worked in the same place and also were in the music biz, so we hit it off. 35 years later, I needed him by my side to make it through this journey. He's one of the good ones. We had a great visit, as always, and it made my day. There was an outside patio that we sat on and talked. I took every moment I could to go out there and sit in the sun. Sometimes, I would ask if the nurses could go out to sit with me because I had a trach tube in my neck. I couldn't be alone out there.

It was so nice now that I was mobile in my wheelchair. I was able to roam the halls and I did all the time. The better I got each day, the further I would go. I could feel my arms getting stronger from pushing myself. And I also realized what type of rehabilitation center I was in. I saw people in all kinds of shape, some not as bad as me, some much worse than me. It gave me a new perspective on life and scared me a little. I knew I didn't want to stay here for very long. I wanted to go home.

I am feeling better, and I can talk better each week, but I want to know if I could sing again. I would go into my bathroom and try to sing a little. It was rough but I could do it. I just had no support because my stomach muscles got cut during surgery, but I kept trying. They were so cool to me here. They would let me use a bathroom up front by the offices and I would play "Patiently" by Journey and sing to it loud as I could.

When I would come out, the office lady was like, "Come back tomorrow." LOL. It was nice to know I could sing but I wanted this thing out of my neck so I could really know what my new sound would be like.

It was about the 3-week mark in this new rehabilitation center, and while it was a great place, I realized that in order to get out of here, there were still a lot of things I needed to have done, doctors to see and business to take care of. I would have to be my own advocate if I was going to keep on schedule.

Every day I would see new doctors and I wasn't sure who did what. Each time anybody came in, I would say, "What about this or this? How do I get my tubes out or get full clearance to use my leg or see an eye doctor to know what's going on with my eyes?" It seemed overwhelming. But be careful what you ask for. The next day, my floor nurse, Boo, who was the best and took great care of me, said, "Hey, I got an order to take out your PICC tube because you take your pills now, so you don't need it."

I said, "Okay, what does that mean?"

She said, "Lay down on your bed, pull up your shirt."

I thought, *Okay*.

She looked at all my tubes and said, "It's this one, Boo. You don't need it so let's get rid of it." She said, "Relax and in your mind go to your happy place."

Hawaii it was.

She said, "Where are we?"

I said, "On the beach."

She said, "Good." Then I felt a tug inside me. She said, "Tell me what it looks like," and I could feel her pulling slowly. It was the weirdest feeling. She was just pulling out a 10-inch tube from inside me. Then at the end, right before it came out, she said, "Are you ready, Boo?"

I said, "Yeah."

She pulled the end out, put a bandage on it but there was no bleeding. How is that? All I could think was, *So I must do those four more times? Oh man, the stress is real*. LOL.

But that is for another time. One down. On to the next hurdle. There were so many things I was dreading, but in order to go home, I had to do them all. It was big boy time. Damn.

The next day, my floor nurse, Boo, was off and my new nurse was here. He was a very cool guy.

He looked more like an MMA fighter then a nurse. He was super funny, and it was a great time when he was on shift. Over time, I really got to like him, and he was a good motivator. I call him the Toe Whisperer, LOL, because I had an injury on my toe that could have cost me my toe. But with a lot of time and attention, the wound nurse and him saved my toe. He was a great sounding board for me and helped me understand the long-term pickle I was in. I just needed to take the bull by the horns and work through it. It was good to be surrounded by people like this. He also helped me keep things on track so I could get out of there.

I remember it was around this time that my son, Josh, was coming to see me, He had not seen me since he saw me in the emergency room. It was very traumatizing for him, and I understood that. I wanted to look the best I could, as healthy as I could so he had confidence that his dad was fine, and I would be home soon. I got dressed and made sure I looked as normal as possible. I took a scarf and put it around my neck so he couldn't see my trach. It looked good.

I had to meet him and his mom upfront in the lobby area. It was nice. They had some chairs and it looked like a waiting room area. I made sure I was already up there when he got there, I moved my wheelchair aside and just sat in a regular chair. It was perfect. When he came in, he saw me, and I stood up and he came over and gave me the longest hug. It was awesome. It felt so good to see him and I know it was a relief for him to see his dad looking so good.

We had a great conversation and laughed a lot and then, of course, my doctor and the floor nurse came to see me. Now this doctor looks like a WWE wrestler and my nurse looked like an MMA fighter, so Josh was not sure what was about to happen. LOL. The doc says, "Jay can you lift your shirt so I can see your tubes?"

And I thought, *Now? Really?* I said, "Josh, look that way." LOL.

This was a good thing because after they left, Josh said, "That's your doctor and nurse?"

I said, "Yeah, crazy right?" But it was nice for Josh to see I was in a cool place and had badass doctors and nurses taking care of me. It made it a little less scary for him and me. LOL.

After this visit, Josh told his mom he felt so much better after seeing me. Mission accomplished. He came to see me whenever he could after that. I love those boys. It helped so much to see them, but also made me want to go home.

I am sort of mobile and, at this point, I am really getting arm strength back. I can cruise around the whole facility, and I did spend time going up and down the halls. But what started to happen when I did that would change my life forever.

I am not on a lot of drugs, like the last place, and I feel like my mind is pretty solid and my reasoning is good. I have been scoring really well on all the memory tests they are giving me. But what started to happen rocked my world a bit.

There was a lady that always sat at the nurse's station at the end of the hall. In order to get to the patio, I would have to pass by her. One day as I rolled by it felt like she was calling out to me, but she couldn't speak. I just started to feel sick and then my head started to hurt, like bad. It was like pressure was building in my head. I quickly rolled by her and the further away I got, the better I felt. I wasn't sure what it was, but I knew it was not me. After a bit on the patio, I had to roll back by her again. As I did, I started to get sick again and my head hurt. She was looking right at me. It was like I could feel what she was going through. It was crazy. I quickly went by and went back to my room to recover. I was sweating. Shortly after, the CNA came in to take my vitals and they were all high. I said try again later. I didn't think too much about it. I just wanted to sleep for a while.

Once I got up, it was dinner time, which I always was up for. The more I was working out and doing therapy, the hungrier I would get. Later that night, I wanted to talk to the boy's mom about what happened that day. I was not sure about telling anyone what happened. I didn't want her to think I was going crazy. She might not bring me home. Now to put things in perspective, the boy's mom, Mariam, is a very smart, together person. She's been in the music biz for over 30 years, is very successful and has seen it all. And she is also into the new age higher learning sort of things. Let's just say she loves Sedona, AZ.

When I told her what happened that day, she was super supportive and reminded me that I had a head injury, and my brain's neurons were reconnecting. There might be a lot of experiences that may happen during my recovery that may seem weird or unusual but try to embrace it. It seemed like there was something she wasn't telling me, but I just let it go. I knew that through this whole process she was giving me the information I needed as I could handle it.

CHAPTER ELEVEN

The next morning, I am up early and I'm trying to shave. It's so weird to have to relearn things you have done most of your life, but I was getting it. I remember looking in the mirror at myself. I was so skinny with a bunch of tubes coming out of me, two of my teeth knocked out and huge scar down the front of me. What a fucking mess! LOL. But no time to be vain. Just heal. I was ready to go once Hannah showed up. We were making huge progress, but it was hard to keep working on one leg because I still had no clearance to put weight on my other leg.

It was around this time that my leg started to feel pretty solid and when I would wheel into the bathroom, I would stand up to pee. I would start to stand on both legs, and they felt strong.

The next doctor I saw, I asked if I could get an x-ray of my hip to get clearance to use my other leg in therapy. I still had a broken collar bone, and it was getting sore from hopping so much on my walker. I just wanted to try to walk with both legs. And again, so many doctors, so many injuries. You have to be your own advocate in recovery to make sure you're moving to the next level of care.

A couple days later, in the middle of the night, some dude wakes me up and says, "Hey man. I must get some x-rays of your hip."

I was like, "Cool, let's do it."

He has a machine that he brings into your room, so you don't have to go anywhere. It was great. I saw his computer screen as he was doing them. I saw a huge screw and some new hardware in my hip. It was like reality set in when you see those things, but that's nothing to what I would see when I went to the doctor's office later. Before he left, I asked, "So how does it look?"

He said, "Well there's no visible fracture left."

I was like, "Yes!"

I couldn't wait to see Miss Hannah in the morning and tell her the good news. I told her to look at the x-ray because I wanted to use my leg, but the dream killer was when she said, "Yes, it does say no fracture, but you need to be released by your doctor before I can let you use it."

I was like, "Come on. It says its healed," but Hannah was a "by the book" kind of girl and I was still too weak to arm wrestle her for it. LOL.

Because I am a bad boy, after she left, I went in my bathroom, stood up out of my wheelchair and walked three steps to the sink. I just started to cry. I knew at that moment I would walk out of that place. It would take a lot of work but eight weeks ago, I was paralyzed, in a coma with pneumonia and now I was walking. It was hard to explain what it was like to fight back from being so broken.

After lunch, it was time for another cruise down to the front and get some exercise before afternoon therapy with April. I was heading back to my room and there was a bit of a traffic jam in the hall. I stopped in front of this guy's room who had two amputated legs and he had his stubs in a duffle bag, which was weird. Then I started to feel odd again. I didn't feel good, but it was different. It was like my mind was getting sucked into his room. I just felt total dread and anxiety. It was so heavy.

I felt so sad and just started to tear up. When a nurse said, "Sorry. Am I in your way?" I couldn't speak. I just rolled out of there fast as I could. I thought, *What the hell is going on? My brain is misfunctioning*. But this felt different. I could swear I was feeling that dude's feelings. It was like I was him for 10 seconds and no thanks. I went to my room. I was sort of scared, like *Damn is my brain ok? how hard did I get hit?* LOL. The brain is a super complex machine, and I am just so glad that my works as well as it does, and I feel normal. My neurologist did say, "It takes the brain a while to heal. During that time, you will experience many sorts of things and out of place memories and you will be emotional. You have been through a lot."

CHAPTER TWELVE

Around this time, I really had to be my own advocate with the business of recovery, everything from insurance settlements to insurance programs. It was a lot. Thank God, again, my son Zack would come to the rehab place and have meetings with me to make sure everything was heading in the right direction.

It seemed I was on a good schedule now. I was getting used to it. Basically, breakfast then therapy then some time on the patio getting some rays. It felt good to have the sun bake on my body, but it also gave me a tan and when my doctors saw me, they would always say, "Well, you're looking really good." LOL.

Little nap in the early afternoon then I would have my Occupational and that meant lots of heating pads which helped me heal faster. If you are a patient in any type of recovery, make sure you take advantage of all your resources.

The next day, Hannah and my afternoon lady came together and said we are doing therapy outside today. I thought, *What's up with that?* But my roommate and I go outside and there are a couple very nice old ladies out there and a board game, Corn Hole, where you throw sand bags through the hole. We did some workout stuff then we started the game. I thought, *This should be easy. I just played this game the day before in therapy.* So, I go, and I do pretty good. My roommate goes. The same. And one lady goes, not too bad. Then this little thing stands up and almost gets a perfect score. She just smiles and sits back down in her wheelchair. I said, "You brought in a ringer," and laughed. I thought, *What has happened to my life? I'm in this crazy rehab place getting my ass kicked by an 80-year-old lady in corn hole. LOL. Man let me heal and get out of here.*

After that abuse, I needed to go for a stroll. I was up front by the office looking at a picture when a younger girl rolled up and said, "Hi, what are you in for?" LOL. I told her and she explained she got sick and now had nerve damage and couldn't really use her legs. She said, "I'm not sure if I will."

I said, "You will. I just know it." But this was one of those weird moments where I could feel it. I knew she would somehow. But this experience was positive. She had a great attitude like I did, so we would meet sometimes in the mornings and chat up life and what it would be like to be on the outside. LOL.

Today, I got news that I was finally getting some things scheduled that needed to happen before I could leave even though I am still a couple weeks out. It felt real that I really might go home and ahead of schedule. In therapy, I was still hopping on one leg with my walker and scooting around in my wheelchair. I was everywhere all the time. I wanted to get out of that bed at 7:00 in the morning and I would get back in late in the afternoon. I was trying to build my endurance. Hannah called this the "spoons theory," whatever that meant. She was kind of a hippy chick so who knows what she was trying to teach me. LOL. But the day after I got home, I knew exactly what she was trying to teach me. It was about not using up all your energy at once. Spread it out throughout the day. See? I was listening.

I knew on Friday I was going to get a CT scan on my stomach. I still had four tubes coming out of me, and I wanted them out. When Friday came. a couple of dudes came into my room with a gurney. They had all my paperwork, so I jumped on. I guess because I still have a trach tube in my neck, they have to transport me by ambulance, so we loaded up.

We went out of the driveway and went up the street, two more driveways and he turned in and said, "We're here."

I said, "Are you freaking kidding me?"

He said, "No, my shortest transport today."

I said, "Man, I could have done this trip in my wheelchair. No wonder my medical bills are over a million dollars. Damn." I did the scan, and it was back to the rehab center. They wouldn't even take me for ice cream for that $1300 trip.

The next day, I saw my WWE doctor guy. He said that he was looking at the scan and there was a 4-inch wide by 8-inch-long piece of hernia mesh down my chest holding my stomach together and he thought he could take out one of my tubes but not the other three. I said, "Okay, when can you do it?"

He said, "Lay back on your bed, pull up your shirt and let me look."

Okay, no sweat. Next thing I know, there's four people around my bed in my room, watching. It felt weird. Guess it looked even weirder. LOL. He just grabbed it and started to pull. You feel it pop off the organ its connected to and then you feel it coming out. No real pain I guess, but you don't want it to happen again. I have three more to go.

CHAPTER THIRTEEN

Every step or procedure means I am one step closer to getting home and that feels good. And I am feeling better. Grandpa says it's about chasing mobility and that's what I am doing each day. I can do something better than the day before and even though I can't work both legs with Hannah because I don't have load baring status, I do work in my room and my roommate cheers me on. I just walk around my bed. It's like musical chairs if someone walks in. I just sit on the bed quick. I had to do what I could. I knew I would not have a lot of time with Hannah and that would be my loss, so I was trying to keep up on my own.

I want to say there were so many heroes that touched my life during my journey and this facility really changed my life. Boo, my floor nurse, was a great inspiration during the day. The other floor nurse, the Toe Whisperer, and all the other amazing people that would help during the day, were really amazing. This is what it takes to heal and recover. I gave up my humility and they gave me back my humanity. Now all the things I couldn't do on my own I can do again. Man, what a hard road.

I could tell that Hannah was ramping up my work outs and homework as I got closer to the finish line. It was getting closer to Halloween. I remember I was feeling so much better, and I was having trouble not walking in front of people so I would often be in trouble. Like on Halloween, they had couple busloads of kids come to Trick or Treat with the patients outside. I wanted no part of that but did take the opportunity to head outside to get some sun. I was down by the fence, a bit away from everyone, and I stood up by the fence. I was just standing there on the phone, and I heard a nurse yell, "Look! Is that Jay standing by the fence?" I thought, *Oh no*, so I slowly walked back to my chair and rolled out of there. LOL.

With not a lot of time left, I still have three tubes the need to be removed, need to get clearance from my orthopedic surgeon and I need the trach tube out of my neck. Oh yeah, I still have double vision, but that will be for when I get out of here. I'll go to the eye doctor myself. It was about this time that I asked to use the shower in my bathroom. That way I just got up in the morning and get ready.

When I woke up, I see I have pulled one of my tubes out my stomach somehow in the middle of the night. I saw it laying on the bed. It freaked me out. I called the nurse in a panic, and she said, "Don't worry." It was ok because I wasn't draining a lot of fluid anymore. Man, never a dull moment. I get ready, jump in the shower, and do everything I need to take care of myself. I am on auto pilot. It felt good to know that when I get home I should be able to do all the stuff to take care of myself.

I can tell there is a lot of activity around me. I know people are trying to get me ready to be released. I ordered a walker to take home but I'm not sure I will use it. It would be nice to have.

I worked with the scheduling lady, and she got me set up for my surgeons next week. I am all set with one week left. I was so excited. My family was ready for this part of the journey to be over. It was hard to believe you can leave on a Sunday morning and you don't come home for three months.

I am enjoying my last week. I have made a lot of friends in here and these are the people that helped me survive. I have so much admiration and love for these guys. A part of me would miss their constant care, but it was time to move to the next level of care: my house.

I think I was set to leave Wednesday the 6th but I had a lot to do. I woke up on Sunday to a great sunny day. The window was open, the sun shining in, and I was packing. One of the CNAs brought me some bags and Mariam was coming with Josh today so they could take some of my stuff home. That way I could just leave on Wednesday without a lot of junk and clothes.

The respiratory therapist walked in and said, "I got orders to take out your trach tube."

I said, "No shit? That's great. When?"

She said, "Lay down on your bed."

Whenever someone said that, I knew I wasn't going to like the next ten minutes. LOL. I was like, *Now? Really? Wow*. The last time they did this it was like being strangled for 15 seconds, so here we go. She undid the strap around my neck, and I felt a puff of air and that was it. She put a band aid over the hole in my neck.

It felt so weird. I couldn't talk at first, but it was out. What a nightmare and now it was gone. I was so happy, I called the boys mom and tried to tell her but could hardly talk. LOL. I'd try later, I guess.

Everyone was happy for me. Every win for me was a win for them. It was great. I was happy to tell Grandpa that night. He was proud of me, but he wanted to make sure I could take care of myself once I got home. I kept thinking, *I am leaving three good meals a day. What I am is nuts.* LOL. I had a great Sunday night, ordered a pizza and watched TV. I was so thankful to see my son Josh that day. He was excited I was getting out. He is not a huge dog lover and had been dealing my dogs for a long time. He was such a trooper. Everyone in the family had their job during this event and I was so proud of everyone. My family was my rock. It was amazing.

CHAPTER FOURTEEN

Monday morning came and Hannah was ready to go. We did our workout and I even trained on some steps. It was great. I felt as ready as I could be at this point. Then the floor nurse said, "Here's your paperwork. Give this to your doctor."

I said, "Okay." I looked on the front page and there was a half-page list of injuries. This was the first time I saw all of the injuries. I had no idea, and it was overwhelming. I started to cry, and Hannah grabbed my shoulder and said, "Dude, you lived through all of that. You have a family to go home to.

It's not about what's on that paper. It's about getting out of here to be with them."

She was right. I pulled up my big boy pants and got ready for my big day of getting my tubes out.

Early afternoon, a nurse pops in and said, "Jay were you in the military?"

I said, "No. Why?"

"There's a dude in full camo waiting with a van to pick you up for your appointment."

I said, "Okay."

I rolled out back and he said, "Sit in front. I'll put your chair back in the rehab."

I said, "Okay," not thinking.

So, it was during this ride I realized a couple things. I had bad PTSD or anxiety about being in a car and he was speeding, cranking his radio and talking about Donald Trump. It was a lot at once. LOL. I said, "Dude, slow down. Calm down. It's my first ride. Let's settle down."

He was like, "Okay. I get it. I am a military vet."

I thought, *Great dude*. We get there and he just looks over and said, "There you go."

I thought, *Where do I go?* This was my first outing by myself with no wheel chair.

"Up the steps and down the hall," he said. LOL.

I made it, somehow. It was weird. I was alone. It seemed odd but I got in to see my doctor. He did all the work on my stomach, and I needed these tubes out.

He walked in and smiled so big. "It's nice to see you standing up. I put a lot of work into you."

I was humbled. This was one of the guys who saved my life. I was like, "Listen. Thank you so much for your great work."

He said, "Well you made me do it twice. I want to read you the list of everything that happened to you."

I said, "Okay, thanks but maybe I shouldn't know."

He said, "It's important. You're the only one who will know if something goes wrong."

"Well, ok."

It was brutal. You really couldn't believe someone could live through that. He said, "You're the Miracle, Jay. Enjoy whatever you do from here."

I was a bit stunned. Then, like every fricking doctor, he said, "Lay back and pull up your shirt." He said, "Why do you still have these tubes in?"

I said, "I don't know. I been asking about it for a while." Then he just starts winding one of the tubes up around his hand, pushes on my chest and says, "You might feel a tug and pop."

I feel it pull off my organ inside me and he just kept winding it up around his hand until it pulled out. Then he does the other one, like its nothing. Meanwhile, I am just humming like, *la de da.*

He then says, "Done. Well, you will probably leak out of these two holes on the way home."

I was like, "Leak what?"

It was so weird, but he put a bandage on and said, "Good. You're doing. Great see you in a month."

I said, "Awesome."

It was great to have that done. I was so happy but yet here I was in the waiting room waiting for my ride back to rehab and it was hard. People there were full of anxiety and pain and sadness. These were tough rooms for me to be in. It felt like I could feel all of it. I went to sit outside. I just wanted to get back to the facility.

I got home late, and my lunch and dinner were there. I ate them both. I was starving from a long day. My floor nurse dude came to see me. He was happy that I got the tubes out and he really helped pull everything together so I could meet my deadline. He knew how bad I wanted to graduate from this place. He was a good guy, and it was always a good time when he was on shift.

Again, I was excited to share the news with family and friends that I made it past another hurdle and tomorrow was it. The last doctor and then home on Wednesday. It felt great to be here.

It was weird to go to sleep with no tubes inside me. I was starting to feel whole again. I was now on my way.

It was Tuesday and I was ready to go in the morning. Today was the orthopedic surgeon who put my hips back together. Now I could get clearance to use my other leg one day before I get released and then I can go to outpatient physical therapy and use it. Hannah came in and just talked me through what questions I needed to ask and got him to sign the form to use my leg. I thought, *I better take my wheelchair this time; don't want to walk into the doctor's office when you want him to release you to use your leg, I guess.*

Once I got there, we did an x-ray downstairs and I waited to see him. His assistant came in and saw me, He had a laptop that he set down. He said, "Man, it's so good to see you. I feel like there was a ton of people working on you last time you saw the doctor." He turned his laptop around and I saw my hips with these huge screws in them. There were two in my left hip and a third that goes from one hip to the other. Nice work. I was in shock really. That's a ton of new hardware. I am like the Bionic Man 2021, version 2.0!

"Listen, whatever it took," he said. I was a total rebuild. He said, "Can you walk?"

I stood up out of my chair and walked around the room

"That's amazing, Jay. So cool."

I said, "I know. Tell the doc thanks so much."

He said, "Cool. You are released from restrictions and can use that other leg now and we will see you in a month." On the way out, the doctor was right there and said, "Jay, keep healing. You're doing great."

I said, "You got it. Nice work."

I was released and had the paperwork. It was really late, and my ride was late so I would get back to rehab late… again. But when I got back, the driver dropped me off up front. He took my wheel chair out but now I didn't need to be in. I pushed my chair back down the hall and as I went by the nurses office, the head nurse came out and said, "Jay is that you?"

I said, "Yes ma'am."

She said, "You look like a visitor."

I said, "Well, I am leaving tomorrow." She gave me a big hug. She runs a great ship and does amazing work with her team of nurses.

I turned and started down my hall to my room and people were like, "Wow, look at you," and then the therapy lady stops me and said, "Ae you cleared to walk?"

I said, "Yeah, just got back from my doctor."

She said, "Nice work, why are you pushing your chair?"

I said, "I am pushing my former self back to my room." When I got by my room, I saw some guys that were also in wheelchairs, and I guess they had never seen me walk. They were like, "Wow! So, you can walk."

I said, "Yeah. That's what they have been teaching me to do this whole time." But it was like I was no longer in the club. They said, "Cool. Good luck."

I was so happy to be back. I was going home tomorrow, and I passed all the tests. Man, I couldn't believe it. What a journey. You never think something like this will happen to you, for sure, but here I am.

I had a great dinner and arranged to have the boy's mom pick me up tomorrow at 1:00pm. I just enjoyed the night and said goodbye to all the night people I would not see any more. It was bittersweet. I knew it would be hard to sleep. Last night of vitals every couple of hours. This was nice but soon I was going to be on my own

The next day it was quiet. I was up early, took a shower and I waited for breakfast. I was getting all packed up when Hannah walked in. It was hard to think I would continue my recovery without this person. She works with tons of people, but she has no idea the impact she's had on me. When I first saw her, I could barely sit up in bed. Now I am walking out of here, no wheel chair, no walker, just the way we planned it all those weeks ago.

She took me into the back room, and we worked on the steps. I would have to face this in a couple hours, so she wanted to make sure I had it. Then we walked back to my room. She gave me all the advice she could and said, “Remember the spoon theory.”

I said, “You’re so crazy.”

She gave me the biggest hug. I think we both cried a little. No one has ever taken me from being so broken to being so much better. She will never understand the impact she had on me. I gave her my info so she could keep tabs on my journey.

Then many people started to come in and I said goodbye. These people are my heroes. You can’t teach people to care. They have to want to, and the people here wanted to. It made all the difference. I also wanted to heal and get better and did the work it took to do that. That also made all the difference and it felt so great.

They give you a walker when you leave. I was joking and said to the lady who orders them, “I need a nice one. Maybe black with flames on it.” She laughed and went on her way. Today, I got an amazon package in my room that said my walker wouldn’t make it today, but here were the flames. LOL. It was some flame stickers for my walker.

LOL. That's going the extra step. This place was great for me for sure.

I was so excited when Mariam finally showed up. I gave her a big hug. She was the other person that went through as much or more than me during this journey. She fought as hard as I did to make sure today was possible. And sure, she's my ex-wife and I am the boy's father, but I have never been so proud of my family. I have to say you never know until something happens, but I was sure my family was there for me, no question. During this journey, I thought a lot about my brother and family back in Iowa. It is so hard to be so far apart during something like this, so I am thankful for all the support and prayers.

ଓଡ

Finally, one of the big wigs from the rehabilitation center came to my room to walk me out and give me my graduation papers. Kick me to the curb! LOL. He walked me up to the nurses were Boo got all my paperwork together and a couple prescriptions I needed to get.

Then it began. So many big hugs from everyone and clapping and laughing and cheering. It was so great. I couldn't believe it. He walked us out to the car, gave me a hug and said, "You did amazing. You are the Miracle."

I said, "Thank you for putting me back together again," and off we went.

Mariam said, "Let's go eat lunch."

I said, "Oh my god, yes please." We went to Culvers and had lunch.

She asked, "How do you feel?"

I said, "Weird." There are so many people out here and so much hustle and bustle for sure, but lunch was amazing. I was free, like getting out of jail. You feel glad to be out, yet you feel out of place, like you're no longer in sync with the rest of the world. It was strange and you just try to take it all in.

CHAPTER FIFTEEN

I made it home and I was amazed I was about to walk up the steps to my apartment I left 3 months earlier. I walked in and it was just like I left it, but it smelled more like dogs then my hospital room. LOL. The boys and their mom filled my fridge with a bunch of food and got me all the supplies I would need for the next couple weeks so I could just relax and heal. The dogs were at Mariam's house, and I was excited to see them, but I was also scared. My one dog, Jett, is a large, powerful Australian shepherd and I was afraid he might hurt me by accident. It was a tough moment to get through. I thanked her so much. She reminded me how important it was that I lived and showed the boys that you can fight your way back from a tragedy like this.

She asked, "Are you ok for a couple hours?"

I said, "Sure." She was going home and would bring the dogs back later with the boys. It would be great to see everyone.

She left and there I was, alone, for the first time in months. It was weird. I took a moment and thanked God again for letting me come back and be with my family. I said I would work hard to recover the best I could for that opportunity. I just sat on the couch watched my own TV, got a drink and something to eat. Wow! I am home. I just couldn't believe it. I was getting dropped back into my life

I was still exhausted and still dizzy, so I was ready for my nap. Later that night, they brought the dogs back. I hide behind the refrigerator so they wouldn't attack me, and I could protect myself. When they came in and saw me, you could see the relief on their faces. They went nuts barking, crying, wiggling all over the place… it was great to see them. I knew they missed me as much as I missed them. It was so good to be home with my family hugging me. This was why I worked so hard to come home. I said they could stay the night then Mom and Josh would come to get them the next morning. I slept great. It was nice to be in my own bed, but it was scary to be alone that first night. In rehab, every couple of hours someone was checking on me, but it's so quiet and so dark. When I got up in the middle of the night, I used my walker to get to the bathroom. I was still so dizzy and unstable. I didn't want any home accidents. I just took my time.

Next day, it was an amazing feeling to wake up at my own house. I lived. I frickin' lived! I went through hell and now I am back. Every day I am so thankful to be alive. I got up but didn't want to risk a shower yet so I got ready and waited for Josh and Mariam to show up to grab the dogs so I could relax my first day. It was nice. I wasn't sure what to do. It was like I said, out of place, so I just did same thing I did in rehab. I said I would keep same schedule so

I could make an easy transition. I did my therapy for the first time without Hannah. It was bittersweet. I was glad to be home, but I did like my support system in rehab.

When I was done, I thought, *Hey, I am gonna go down and check my mail.* Seemed easy, so I walked downstairs very carefully, and I started to head past my parking space, and I was wasted. I was so tired. I stopped, and, in my head, I heard that crazy Hannah's voice trying to explain the spoon theory. I laughed and said, "Oh, this is what she's talking about." LOL. Don't try to do too much too fast. Space out your energy… yada yada… LOL. Man, I was dusted. I was thinking, *Damn, how will I get back upstairs?* LOL.

How can this be? I just leaned up against a poll for a bit then made my way back upstairs. Once I got there, I went right to bed, turned on TV and just relaxed the rest of the day. That's when I realized it was going to still take a long time to heal. Just because I was home didn't mean I wasn't still really injured. It was hard to take but I realized that changing locations just meant a new level of care and I needed to get a program in place quick.

It's funny. Dogs are so smart, for sure. The kind I have are very smart. They could tell I was very injured and were tip-toeing around me. But Willow, my girl, she is super smart. When I was laying on the bed, she came up on the bed and just started to sniff all my broken parts. She was super sniffing my hips where I have new hardware. Then she just laid down with her head over my leg. She looked sad or maybe disappointed in me like, "What did you do and where have you been?" Poor girl. LOL. Jett was my struggle. I needed to be able to take him out and walk him, so I needed to get better quick.

These are the things that help me survive and also heal quicker:

- Be positive. Have a plan of recovery. Have a plan of action. Body scan every night to focus your body on the high trauma areas. Do your physical therapy every day, twice if you can.

- Increase mental health. Laugh and be happy however you can.
- Reach out to people. I thought it was so cool that my school mate Mark checked in with me on Facebook every week while I was in rehab. So cool. Just stay connected to your reason to survive.

CHAPTER SIXTEEN

So, it's day two and I realize I need to take it nice and slow, but I wanted to get out and start to walk. After I got up and ate some breakfast, I wanted to take a walk. I texted Mariam and told her, "This is what I am doing," so we always knew where I was just in case. I was dying to get to my art studio in the garage just to take a look, see how it looked after three months. Prior to my accident, I was on a creative streak. I did tons of art and made four different calendars to sell on my website. It was like my body knew I was about to go into hibernation for a while, so it needed to get all this work done.

But now I was wondering if this was something I could still do or would want to do. I knew it was great therapy. I grabbed the remote and off I went again. It was just nice to be walking outside. My garage is not super close, but I made it. When the garage door went up, it was like a wave of emotion. It was great to be back in the studio. This is who I am, a creative person making art, making music. This is what someone stole from me, and I was here to claim it back. I am not a patient anymore. I need to transform back into myself. It was the last step of this journey, to try to become who I was before the accident or as close as possible. I knew I was not the same person, so I just wanted to put the pieces of the puzzle back in place and slowly build myself around those pieces, like my family.

It seemed stuffy, like no one had been in here in months, but it was so bright. The colors seemed so much brighter as I sat and went through my art, and it was so cool how I looked at them now. Before, I was just like a machine pumping them out now. I was an observer, checking them out. It gave me another perspective and maybe will make me better at this. I just had the music on, and I was cleaning and people who used to see me in here every day started to stop by and ask where I have been, what happened. It was a lot and still hard to talk about, but it was nice that people missed me and were watching out for me.

ଛଚ

As I sat there, I realized I had so much to take care of and so much healing yet to do but it was a beautiful day in Arizona, and I was out like a normal person. It was nice. I made it back upstairs, but I was beat. I had some lunch then went to bed to sleep. My body would always tell me what it needed so I just listened at this point. I was good at doing what I was told. I never took so many orders in my life. LOL.

I relaxed for the evening, and I knew I had a in home nurse coming to see me and doing a home check to make sure everything was safe at my house, to see how I was on my own. The next morning, I got ready for her to come. The dogs were at the boy's house. I was still having double vision and needed to go to my ophthalmologist next week. The nurse shows up and she says, "Wow, you're Jay?"

I said, "Yes."

She said, "I read your report. I was expecting someone in much worse shape. You look good."

I said, "Well I am trying. It's been a long road, but I got this." I noticed she had on super thick glasses which I thought was odd.

She did my exam and, yeah, it's weird getting an exam in your living room, but this was my new normal. She said everything looked great. I said, "Well I still have double vision. Not sure what they will do about that."

She said, "I have had double vision since I was a kid. That's why I have these glasses. They're there called prism glasses."

I said, "Wow, really? So, you can see fine with them?"

She said, "Yeah. But you don't want to get them if you can help it. They make your eyes weak and now I need them all of the time." I thought, *Crap how will I navigate this issue? I have to see again.*

At this point, I had no idea what was up with my eyes. No doctors would even give me an opinion. After she left, she said I needed to go see my primary care doctor. I made an appointment for the next week. I had a lot of people yet to see so I would go to a doctor or two a week for the next six months.

Right now, I am scheduling for a week at a time, but I am taking it one day at a time, nice and slow. Every day I feel better, but I can tell this will take a long time. My mom was right. She said, "Your vessel is so broken it will take a long time to heal." She was right. But it was about my new normal and my fight for mobility. I called this physical therapy place across the street from my house. I knew I had to start eight weeks of therapy and I wanted to keep going from where Hannah and I left off. I was able to get in the next week, so not much time off. I wanted to gain weight and build muscle so I signed up and I could walk or maybe ride my bike? I was starting to build my new health network around my neighborhood, all the places I would need to go but I could get to them quick by Uber or bike or walk.

A couple days later, I started therapy. I took my walker and walked across the street just to be safe, but it was pretty close. Cool, I could do this. I signed in and had my evaluation and explained my situation. The doctor was great. I felt like I was in the right place.

Then he said, "The folks in the back will give you your first hour session."

I was like, "Cool." I go back and these two girls come over and I say, "Hi, I am Jay."

They say they were the Hannah's. I said, "Say what?"

She said, "Both our names are Hannah."

I said, "Wow. My last therapist's name was Hannah," and they laughed. I continued, "Man, one was bad enough now I have to put up with two of you." LOL. Maybe it was fate, but I could tell we were ramping up from my old workouts. This would be a tough eight weeks. I wanted to test my mobility as soon as I could. My goal was just to take walks again at night with the dogs.

The walk there and back was a lot so when I went by my garage, I stopped in and got my bike out. I have a bad ass mountain bike that I've had a while but never really used. I thought if I can ride this, it would give me a way to exercise and also expand my mobility area. I grabbed it, brought it outside the garage, got on it and sort of just held myself up. If I was going to try this, I needed to make sure I could do it. I was only home a week. If I crashed, everyone would kill me. But then, I used to jump over kids with my skateboard when I was a little kid. Surely I got this. LOL.

I push off and I am riding nice and slow. It felt pretty good and actually didn't hurt as bad as walking. I went around the parking lot a little and then back to my garage. Okay, I did it. I think I could do this. Man, I hope so. I didn't want to do something stupid that could set me back again.

CHAPTER SEVENTEEN

It's time to go see my primary doctor. He has been my doctor for like seven years. I like him, and I trust him. The last time I saw him was a week before my accident. We did some tests and he said I needed to lose some weight and eat better. I said, "No sweat," then not less than a week later I have my accident. So here I was not looking that great and about to see him for first time in three months.

I gave the nurse my list of injuries when I got there. I told her what happened so he would have a little background before I saw him. She put me in a room, and he knocked and comes in and says, “Jay, what happened to you?”

I said, “Didn’t you tell me to lose some weight? Well, I lost 30 pounds.”

He laughed and said, “No, not like this.”

I explained what happened and he was amazed that I was alive. And wasn’t very happy I road my bike there to see him. LOL. I said, “Listen, I have to get mobile.”

He said, “I can’t get behind that yet. Just Uber around.”

I was not getting a lot of support for my bike riding at this point, but I understand. No one wanted to see me get hurt again so I was very careful.

We got a game plan to get me back on track. What was funny was I was in a rehabilitation center in Peoria, and I guess my doctor sees some of his patients there, but I never ran into him. Weird. You would think when you get nailed like I did they would contact your primary care giver and say, “Hey we got one of your patients here and he’s a mess.” But who knows. Makes too much sense, I guess.

Every day I could feel I was getting better and the things that were not getting better started to stand out. It's crazy when you have so many injuries. You're always in pain and then there are moments when I don't have any pain and it's unbelievable. But there is one thing that is driving me crazy now: my eyes. I still have double vision and it's making me crazy. I set an appointment with my ophthalmologist for the next week. I had so many doctors to see. The boy's grandpa helped me get a game plan to see one doctor a week for the next few months. It would keep a better handle on my recovery. One thing at a time. He was right. It made my recovery not so overwhelming in the long run.

ᏅᏕ

For the next week, I would keep my same schedule as I did in rehab but better because I was at home. LOL. I get up, get ready for the day, go to therapy then go to the gym to work out then take my bike ride. The weights are light, the reps are small, and the rides are short. My goal is to ramp up every week for the next year. I knew at this point it would be a year of this same schedule, so I was committed to taking advantage of great advice, expert instruction, and amazing family support to maximize my recovery results.

I am ready to Uber to my eye doctor. I can't wait to find out what's up with my eyes and thank God for Uber. My family is there when I need them, but I am trying to be independent, to do things on my own. They have been troopers for months, but I want to get my life back.

I meet my eye doctor and he does a bunch of tests. The bottom line is not good news. I had a head injury and had a damaged sixth cranial nerve. The only job this nerve has is to pull the eye back in place and it's not working right at the moment. He said it could take months to correct itself. If not, I would need eye surgery to pull the muscle back in place. I said, "Great. So, I can't drive until this heals."

He said, "Not right now anyway."

It was a long ride home. I was devastated to think that maybe I would never drive again. It was a rough pill to swallow but I had to stay positive. I still had a few months, and I would need to concentrate my healing efforts to my eyes now I knew what the problem was. It was time to work with my body to heal it. I watched so many videos on eye therapy and double vision. Man, you could drive yourself nuts! But I needed to get educated on my injuries so I could be my own advocate to get these injuries fixed.

Every week I get a grip on my new reality, my new normal, and now I realize that the doctor's work is done for the most part. We will have a tune up here or there, but for the most part the physical shape of my body is up to me. If I want to be in great shape, I will have to work for it. I was a mess, but I knew I could do it. I just needed to keep up the hard work. I am not going to lie. I am scared to death. I wonder at this point what will not work out for me no matter how much I try; I am lucky, but not win the lottery lucky, so I am hoping for the best.

Like always in this journey, I let the boy's mom know what the news was on my eyes, and she always puts a positive spin on everything. I was a prisoner to time with a lot of my injuries. I would just have to wait and see.

I have been out of rehab and hospitals for about a month and it's hard to get back to my normal life. I just thought of my life as an extension of rehab: keep doing all the rights things and space out the high trauma points.

Today I was seeing my orthopedic surgeon. I have been doing great in therapy and I am feeling better about the way I walk. It should be good appointment. I hope I get to meet the guy who put me back together. I walked into the waiting room and, sure enough, my surgeon walks in with his assistant.

I stood right up, walked over and shook his hand. He smiled so big and said, "Man, look at you. It's amazing." He gave me a hug and I said, "Dude, thank you so much for your great work."

He said, "I am gonna tell you something. When I was working on you, I always thought you would live but there were skeptics who said, 'Why are you putting so much effort in on him? He may not wake up.' But I work on people like they are all gonna wake up and look at you, my proof. I did go by you every day in the emergency room, and I would look in and see you with that tube in your mouth and I would think wake up man."

I said, "Man you should of said it a little louder." LOL.

He said, "Seriously, you are the Miracle."

I said, "I hear that a lot. Think I'll write a book called that.

He said, "You should, Jay/ Really do it."

I said, "Okay, I will."

He was a young hip doctor. You could tell he was great at what he did. His patients in the waiting room all rave about how he's the guy but he's also a great human. That's what makes him great. He said, "Come see me right before your year anniversary. Get as mobile as you can before that date because after that it gets harder."

I said, "Okay. Cool."

Again, it was cool to see this guy. I want to meet as many of my heroes as I can. I want to thank all the people that saved my life that day. It's an important part of the healing process to make amends with all the people that helped me along this journey. And it's important to understand that these folks are people too. It's nice to get personal insight on what I went through and how serious my accident was because it's just wrong that your surgeons are so excited to see you alive. They're like, "Wow I did it again." LOL. It's cute to watch but it also drives home I almost died that day. Damn.

It was the holidays, and I was just so grateful to be home with my family and friends. It was nice to hear at the dinner table on Thanksgiving that everyone was so thankful that I was finally home and getting better. Family is so important to the recovery process, and I knew it was great to see my family feeling better. And I am not gonna lie. I totally cleaned up at Christmas. I got everything I wanted and more. LOL. But there was nothing like that morning just watching them open gifts. It was the reason I lived. I want to see more of these moments. I am glad I did not give up and very glad they didn't give up on me.

And we were falling into a routine, Mariam or the boys would take me shopping every week, so I had food and whatever I needed until I got more mobile.

The next day is Saturday and Mariam is going to get new glasses and asked if I want to tag along so I can get out a bit. I said, "Yes please. Come get me. Take me anywhere." I am sitting out front just chilling, waiting for her, and a lady comes and sits a chair away from me. Remember that strange feeling I had at the rehab center whenever I wheeled past that woman? It started again, like I am not feeling well, and it's hard. I feel so sad, and I could tell she had been crying. I could feel how sad she was. I got up went outside and got some fresh air. This really freaked me out. I keep think something is wrong with me but it's them. How is this happening? I feel fine outside so I go back in and sit next to her, and it starts again. Now. I want to cry, and I am about to. I get up and leave, go back outside. Now I know something's up. I could feel what that chick was feeling, and I don't need that to ever happen again. I am not saying anything to Mariam. I needed to research this on my own. But I just keep thinking I lived, and I feel like I just need to let my brain heal more. This may take a while.

The one thing I have said a couple times in this book is I am amazed at how complex the human body is and the brain is a very amazing and fragile machine. If you think about it, most people have five senses. Some have less but do some have more? I guess we're about to find out.

I spend that night online watching videos on my phone of this very thing. I couldn't believe it, and I can say from watching these, it made me feel so much better. So many things during this process made me feel like I was crazy and one by one, I try to figure them out so I can keep using stupidity as my excuse and that I am not crazy. LOL.

Now that I know these things happen, and many people have experienced this, I will need to research it more and figure out if this is a short-term issue from my head injury or will this be a new tool for my toolbox of life. Let's hope I heal my way out of this one.

Every day I am learning more about what happened to me. I am learning my new normal and what my limitations are and also what new limitations I have. It's quite the puzzle to put back together.

I am working very hard right now. My whole life is about getting better and gaining weight and gaining more muscle back. I need to feel unbroken.

CHAPTER EIGHTEEN

It was time to go see my stomach surgeon one last time so I can get cleared from him. I was off to get a CT scan of my belly area. This was one area that still feels super weird. I know I have mesh implant in there holding things together.

The lady who did my scan was the same lady who did it two weeks before my accident. She was like, “Oh hi. Are we doing the same scan as last time?”

I said, “Yeah, but we are looking at something different.”

She was like, "Okay." After the scan she asked, "Jay, what happened? You have a lot more hardware.

I laughed and said, "I went with the upgrade." I told her the story she was so sorry and was glad I made it out alive.

The next day I was off to my surgeon. Turns out he was not there, but his assistant was, and we had a scan to make sure there was no fluid left that needed to be drained. If there was, they would have to put tube back in, so I was stressed. She came in and said, "Hey, Jay. Everything looks great. No fluid so that's good." I was so relived. I just wanted to move on. She said, "You're all set. Call us if you have pain or need us."

Man, it felt so great to be cleared from that doctor. Every week I was making progress to getting back to my new normal.

I was feeling better, and it was the weekend. My buddy George came to take me out to dinner. It was so good to talk with him. He was always a good sounding board for me, and he was there from the day of my accident. He had good insight on how I was really doing. You can only hope people like George and my family realize how much you appreciate them being there for you.

Every week I was trying to see a doctor and get to all the things I needed to fix. This week I was going to see my dentist so we could see what it would take to fix the teeth that got knocked out during the crash.

This was big for me because it was one of the last things on the list to get fixed. It had been a long haul, but here I was. The doctor came in and he has been my dentist for about 18 years. W we had been through a lot when it comes to my teeth, my many implants and other craziness. When he came in, he was so happy to see me. He asked me to tell the story of my accident, which was still hard to talk about, but he was so supportive, and it was time to take a look.

Because the teeth were broken off at the gum line, the only choice was to pull a couple and do implants in that area. Not what I wanted to hear but it's what needed to happen. I made quick work of getting over to my implant surgeon. This is another guy I have been going to for many years. He has done all my implants and he's the best so I trust he will do what I need.

I saw him the next week and he was also so sorry to hear what happened to me. I know we all want to get me back to as close to normal as we can. I scheduled surgery for a couple weeks out so I could get all the premeds I need. Now, because I have titanium parts in my body, I have to take special meds before surgery, so all my parts get along and no infections settle in. This is the new protocol for everything in my new world.

Remember, every day starts the same: down to the gym for a workout then for a bike ride. I try to keep mobile and try to get stronger every day. It's my job right now to get in the best shape I have been in for a long time.

Every week I feel better. There are less parts sticking out and bothering me. I want to make a full recovery but that might not be in the cards. I need to be mentally prepared for each new week's challenges.

I have been in my studio everyday creating new art. This is great therapy for me. It's like my brain is stuck on wide open. I just can't stop being creative, so I just keep painting. Then I take high quality photos of my prints and I do a TikTok before adding them to my website. It seems I am busy all the time and I have also started writing this book. I spend a couple hours a day on it. I understand now why my doctors said it would be a great idea for me to write a book. It's sort of a journal of all the things I went through. It helps me to leave the pain on the paper and try to move on from victim to normal person again. I need this help right now. When I got a referral from my doctor to see a therapist, someone who could help with my PTSD or anxiety about my accident, they wanted to do some tests, but insurance denied me. I guess they are trying to curve the amount of money they are spending on me.

I went online and tried to find someone who could help me as well as help me understand some of the crazy things that have been happening to me. I found someone online that seemed to be the right fit. I called her office and the assistant said that the doctor was full and not taking on new patients at this time, but she would take my information and call me. I explained my story to her and about my car accident and the type of things that have been happening to me.

She said, "Okay, great we will let you know."

I started to think about how hard it has been to get help; they will spend over a million bucks to fix this old body but not a dime to make sure I am of sound mind. And if you have been in an accident or have trauma of any kind, you know the anxiety is real.

The next afternoon, I get a call from the doctor's assistant, and she said that the doctor would give me a few sessions at a very reduced rate if that would help me out. I said, "Wow, great. Why?"

She said that the doctor liked my story and wanted to help. Okay, great. I set a time for the next day to speak with her over the phone. The next day, when she called, I knew right away I was speaking to a very educated and savvy lady. She seemed to be at the top of her game, and it really put me at ease.

She asked me to tell my story about the accident which I did. Of course, she was very sympathetic and insightful about what happens when the body suffers severe trauma and also how having a traumatic brain injury can play into your recovery process. This lady was on fire, so smart. But then she said, "Tell me the story of when you think you felt someone else's pain."

I thought, *Oh no she is gonna hang up on me*. LOL. I told her about the different times this happened in the rehab center and also when I got out.

There was a bit of silence before she said, "Wow. You are amazing. It sounds like you are an empath."

I said, "A what?"

She said, "Yes. It sounds like you are an empath. An empath is someone who is highly aware of the emotions of others around them to the point of even feeling those emotions themselves." She continued, "Empaths see the world differently than other people. They are highly aware of others, their pain points and what that person might need emotionally."

Now I was silent.

She said, "Jay?" LOL.

I said, "Sorry. Are you kidding me? This is a thing? How would this be possible really?"

She said, "Well, you have aways been a caring, empathetic person, I am sure, and sometimes when you get a brain injury like you did it, can affect your pineal gland in your brain. It's called your third eye and its where all these emotions and empathetic thoughts come from. Yours could be stuck on open because of your injury and now you are not able to control what type of insight you are getting from people."

I said, "So, when I was in rehab, and I could feel the pressure in that lady's brain, that was me feeling her pain?"

She replied, "Yeah. You were taking on her pain, but it can also be happiness. It's really any strong emotion someone is having. You could take on that emotion."

I said, "That seems impossible.

She said, "When you see someone throw up, does it make you want to throw up?"

I said, "Yeah.

She said, "So that's the most basic example of this gift. Everyone has it to some extent but for some reason, yours has amplified into another sense that you can learn to use. Many people have five senses and they have defined them. There are people that have more than five senses because they have defined and mastered them just like their other senses."

But I am not sure. I said, "Why would someone want to feel someone else's pain? I can tell you it's not that great of an experience."

She laughed and said, "I understand but like any gift, once you learn to use it and define it, there are many good things that can come of it. But first you need to control it and shield yourself when you don't want it to happen." She continued, "Go online and watch some videos on this subject and try to wrap your head around this new change you are going through. Just know you are not crazy. You are gifted and as you heal, your mind, and body, will feel more solid. Let's talk again next week."

The first thing I thought was how nice it was to get some solid advice on my mental state from my accident. She helped me deal with the trauma and she said it can get trapped in my nervous system. I would have to learn to release it and then the pain of what I went through. Slowly it would go away. And writing this book would be the best therapy I could get.

I was a little shocked to hear what else she had to say but I would have to investigate this more. Maybe this is something that will go away as my brain heals. I'm not sure, but again, I'm glad I am not crazy.

I spent the next week watching tons of videos and other people who claim to have similar experiences. I guess it makes simple sense that if you are a person who has empathy for people and all things, and you are connected to your own emotions, that you could at least sympathize with other people because you have a broader understanding of that arena. I think this is complicated for me. I just want to heal and get in great physical and mental shape. I can do without getting in an Uber and feeling that my driver is super depressed or needs to get his heart checked because I can feel his chest is tight and now my chest is tight. It's like, *Really? Damn, I just need a ride to Target, man.* LOL.

I can feel each week. I am feeling better. I am working on the parts that still hurt the worst. Some I can't do much about, like my ribs. I am finally able to roll over a little on my side at night but just my right side. I broke most of my ribs on the left side and it's still hard to lay on them. Plus, I broke the left collar bone, so it will be a year before I can think about it. It's weird to think about your recovery at the one-year mark. Everything we are doing is judged by how I feel at the one-year anniversary of the accident.

But so many of you reading this right now know that time is your friend when you are healing. Time is never really on our side during recovery. It seems it's always illusive. Everyone just keeps saying it takes time but how long? No one really seems to know. So, the journey is forever as long as you are always trying to be better than you are right now.

ᘓᘐ

I have a big week. I am still busy seeing doctors every week so up this week is implant surgery. My son Zack is taking me and then getting me back home. He has been such a trooper for me during this journey. The surgery goes great because this guy is really good, and I am not going to lie. I was nervous. This was my first time getting put under, so I wanted to make sure I woke back up. But it was great. His staff was amazing as always and the girls there are so nice. Zack got me home and poured me into bed and I was out for the day.

This week was also my eye doctor. Right now, this is a tough one, man. I just don't seem to get better. It's like I think it's getting better but he's saying I am finding ways to cheat and see around the problem. I really don't want eye surgery, believe it or not, so I need to just keep positive and work on my eyes at night. He said maybe I can try eye therapy. It might help but he doesn't seem to think it will change my world that much. This gets me. Your vision is so important, and I can think of other problems I would trade it for.

But I guess that's not how it works.

CHAPTER NINETEEN

I am feeling better that each week, I am clawing my way back to being healthy again. Now during this process, the police department and county attorney have kept in touch with me and keeping me updated on my criminal case with the drunk driver who hit me. These are always tough moments because I just want to get better. I don't want to be reminded that I was a victim of a crime, but I know it's also part of my healing process. They ask your opinion of what should happen to him as far as his sentence and jail term.

I try to work through that process with forgiveness and understanding. No doubt, he F'd up both of our lives, but I just need to keep rocking and focus on my recovery not his punishment. The key is to think about what I have gained back since this incident, not what I have lost because of it. But Glendale, AZ, has done a great job of making sure there will be justice for my near-death experience, and I am sure this guy and myself will have a new outlook on life because of it.

It's been months since my accident. It is hard to try to get back to normal. My life right now is still about recovery. I hate being a victim, so I am trying to just get back to the things in life that make me happy and feel normal, like my art and my music. The art is no problem but when I try to sing now, it's rough. It makes me sad, and I hope I didn't lose that gift. It sucks but I will start over and keep at it.

I have my last therapy session with my doctor, and she is awesome. It's nice to get some validation about how my brain is also recovering from the accident and how there is a real science behind what I am going through. Each week is about coming closer to my new normal. I told her I would like to give some of my art to my physical therapist, Hannah, to thank her for helping me walk again. She thought that was a great idea. So, after a couple weeks of trying to coordinate our schedule's, Hannah was able to stop by my studio after work one night. It was great to see her. It had been about six months since I got out and I was 130 pounds when I left. Now, I am 155 and have been in the gym for months so I know I looked a little different.

She said, "Wow! You look great!" and that's what I wanted to hear from her. I was trying to make her proud for months. All of her hard work had paid off. Good for her.

We talked for a while about my experience and what's next for me and then she facetimed her boyfriend. They went shopping, picking a couple prints they really liked. I was so glad to give them to her. It was like a very small payback for what she had done for me. It was a healing moment for both of us.

I was able to thank her for what she did for me, and she was able to see how her hard work paid off.

I noticed during this process there were doctors and nurses and others that truly love helping people and you getting better is part of their payoff and reward. These people are the compassion of our health care industry. It was hard to say goodbye to her. We took pictures and hugged. I knew that she could tell I was far less broken than I was before and that was a cool moment for me. We will stay in touch, and we will cross paths again on this journey, but I am glad that she touched my life and had such an impact on me.

The next day, Hannah texts me and said she loved her new art, and I was very happy. I woke up feeling like I had moved to the next level of recovery.

ଓଡ

Like I mentioned earlier, the Maricopa County prosecutor's office has been keeping me up to date on the guy who hit me and what was happening with his court case. They of course ask my opinion of what should happen to him, what I would like to see him get for jail time and other things. I have to say this is a hard process to get through. On one hand, I forgive this dude, yet I want to make sure I am his only victim. Because I did not see him coming when he t-boned me at 57 miles per hour and pushed my car across the intersection and into two more cars, I don't remember anything from that accident. But it was hard to read the reports of what other people saw at the accident scene. It didn't look good for me, for sure, but thank you to those people that were there and tried to help.

I know that this experience has changed my life. I hope that whatever journey this guy has to take now, he will learn his lessons and will be successful in changing his life as well.

I will say the most out of body experience that occurs from super high impact trauma is the inability to believe that this happened to you. I thank God that time would slowly pull me over the hump of recovery.

I will say again that I know my mom is still close to me. Ever since I woke up from a coma, I would dream about my mom every six weeks or so. But it was always like she was in another room talking to someone, but I couldn't really make out who it was or what they were saying. As I heal, I start to hear the dreams better. She is always talking to someone, telling them how she feels I am doing in recovery. She always says, "But he is so stubborn. I am not sure he will do it," and the male voice says, "I know he can." I think, *Damn mom, give me some slack.* LOL. I cannot tell who this male person is but it's always the same voice.

I guess I understand there are more than just people helping me. The struggle is real. The fight is hard. And the recovery is long. You just can't do it alone. I am not sure what is happening, but I am glad to be in good company.

ꝏ

I was finally feeling more like myself and had more things in the rear-view mirror. I know there is still a long road ahead of me but the small wins, like having good days and progressing through things, gives you hope. I know I am back in charge of myself, making my own decisions and carving my own new path. And as time goes on, I am getting stronger, and my body looks like it's in shape. You would not be able to pick me out of a line up as the guy who got crushed.

But it's more of a mask or façade. I realize that I won't be like I was before. I can't do things like I did before. It's much better than everyone thought, and you don't know if there will be any setbacks, like my eyes. I just take it week by week and then month by month. Whatever my new normal will be, I'll find it and I will build around it.

Mariam, the boys' mom, keeps saying, "You don't know how much you have changed." She said, "You don't sweat the small stuff and things that use to aggravate you no longer bothers you."

I said, "Well, for sure, I have found my new inner peace. I know now what life is about and what our mission here is and how we are supposed to act and most important how we should treat others" Anyone can have a better life. It's not about changing your life. It's about changing your focus. Our souls only come here to be educated on the lessons we are supposed to learn. It's important not to be sidetracked.

It's almost the one year anniversary of my accident. I am seeing a lot of my doctors and I'm still in physical therapy for my shoulder. Soon, I will have my teeth put in one, of the last physical things you can see.

My eyes are still in question. They have gotten a lot better but are still changing on me so this will be my long-term issue to deal with.

I just saw my orthopedic surgeon for my one year visit. I really like this guy. He did a great job on me and when I walk in to see him, I can tell I was a project, and he is proud of his work. LOL. I was so lucky to have guys like this on my team. He installed a lot of new hardware in my hips. It's monsoon season and I can feel it. But he said, "Same time next year." It's nice to move appointments to yearly and not weekly.

I was released by my dental implant surgeon to get my teeth restored over the next couple of weeks. Again, this is a great guy to have on my team. He always keeps my best interest in mind, and I always have a good time when I go see him. He has a great staff and I'll be glad to get this finished.

ঔ

LAST TIP: LIFE FOCUS

Change your life focus.

It's not "how can I enhance my life?" It's about "how can I enhance the life of others." Always think about how your actions will influence others. Live with good intentions. Bring positive energy to everything you do and everyone you do it with. Shifting your positive thoughts to others allows positive thoughts from others to affect you. Don't think about what you can't do. Focus on what you can do. Every day is a gift. Use it that way.

So far I am doing it. You can do it to. Is it easy? No, no it's not but it's worth it. If you are recovering from any kind of trauma or life altering experience, it turns out there's only one person who can really make the difference in your recovery. That's you.

There I said it.

It's so true that we have the help of the best doctors and nurses and therapists, but if we don't do what they say, or don't put in the work it takes to get better, guess what?

We don't.

My name is Jay Neyens.

I am now 57 years old. I survived a horrific car accident 11 months ago. I spent three months in the hospital and several months in outpatient rehabilitation and therapy. Now I have a pretty strict workout schedule and bike riding regimen I do every day. For the most part, my body is still healing and getting better. I am getting my dental work finished from getting my teeth knocked out in the accident. I still can't drive because my eyes are still healing.

But I lived.

And I spend my days trying to find out what my new normal is and what the purpose of my second chance at life is.

It has been an amazing past year. I still can't believe this happened to me and changed my life this much. I again have to thank God and my family and friends who got me through this journey and all the amazing health care workers who played a part in my recovery and continue to help me in this endless journey.

I cannot do some things now that I could before the accident. But now I can also do some things I couldn't before the accident. It has been a give and take for me, and I am thankful that I can share my experience and journey with you. I hope there was a part of my story that helps motivate or inspires you to take your journey to the next level.

Because just when you think it can't get any worse… It doesn't.

ABOUT THE AUTHOR

Even as a young kid growing up in a small Midwest town, I knew that I would have to live a creative life. Growing up playing in local bands I knew I found my calling.

Leaving for a vocal school in LA at age 18, I knew this would be a tough choice. I would have to leave my family to chase my dreams. After graduating Outstanding Vocalist later that year, I showed all my hard work had paid off. Playing with some amazing local and national music groups, I found my dreams were now reality.

During this amazing time, I was given a great opportunity to get into the movie and TV business doing special effects – wind, rain, fire, explosions. I was so lucky to work on tons of movies, TV shows and music videos. I had the chance to work on everything from the first *Blade* movie to *MAD TV and* worked with everyone from Cher to Michael Jackson.

Let's just say life got a bit crazy. I wanted to get married and settle down. I moved to Arizona where I had a great life. owned some businesses and had amazing twin boys. Even though my marriage did not work out, I have a great friend and the best kids ever.

But August 15, 2021, I would have a life altering event that would find me fighting for my life. I have documented the next year of my life in the book you are holding in your hands.

Now, my mission is to share my story, help inspire and motivate people. I also use my new gifts to help elevate and guide people through their traumatic experiences as a trauma healer.

I am also an artist. Since my release from the hospital, I have painted every day and hope that I create art pieces that will bring smiles to those around the world.

BE CREATIVE.

CPSIA information can be obtained
at www.ICGtesting.com
Printed in the USA
BVHW051358030123
655316BV00008BA/282